A Brief History of the Organization

A Brief History of the Organization

◆

From The Dawn of Civilization To Leadership of Today's Corporation

Lynn Bentley

iUniverse, Inc.

New York Lincoln Shanghai

A Brief History of the Organization
From The Dawn of Civilization To Leadership of Today's Corporation

iUniverse, Inc.

For information address:
iUniverse, Inc.
2021 Pine Lake Road, Suite 100
Lincoln, NE 68512
www.iuniverse.com

ISBN: 0-595-27132-4

Printed in the United States of America

Contents

PROLOGUE 1

INTRODUCTION 5

CHAPTER 1   PREHISTORIC ORGANIZATION 9

CHAPTER 2   SOCIAL THEORY 14

CHAPTER 3   DAWN OF THE 20TH CENTURY 21

CHAPTER 4   THE MODERN ORGANIZATION 28

CHAPTER 5   THE MODERN ERA 41

CHAPTER 6   EFFECTIVE ORGANIZATION. 51

CHAPTER 7   CEO EXPERIENCE 62

CHAPTER 8   SOCIAL CONNECTION. 80

CHAPTER 9   SCIENCE BRANCHES REUNIFICATION. . . 88

CHAPTER 10   EFFECTIVENESS MODEL 103

EPILOGUE 107

BIBLIOGRAPHY. 115

Acknowledgements

This project was made possible, in part, by the support of several of my business partners with The Curtiss Group International and most importantly our Founder, William E. Frank, Jr. for which I am truly grateful. Special thanks to my extremely able business intern at the Curtiss Group over the last two years Stacy Pagano for her ingenuity and attentiveness. Also, Dorothy Bentley for her exceptional technical support and willingness to act as a pragmatic sounding board!

A number of people—friends, relatives, business associates, and scholars—read and commented on drafts: Douglas Adams, William Anthony, Meghan Bentley, Joseph Cosentino, Lori Hill, and George Milne. All contributed valuable insights and remarks. I also thank the executives that spent time with me reviewing their corporate applications including, Jack Blaeser, CEO, Concord Communications, John Jastrem, CEO, Rapp Collins, Tim Kardok, CEO, Urecoats, Rahul Khanorkar, SVP, Equitrac Corporation, George Milne, recently retired Pfizer Corporate Officer, Carlos Palomares, Chairman, Citibank Latin America, Bruce Rusch, now CEO, Oracom, Ray Sansouci, now CEO, MicroESystems. Their attention to fundamentals led to the development of many of the ideas expressed by me in this project.

Finally, I dedicate this book to my wife Dorothy and my two daughters Meghan Bentley and Lori Hill. They supported my change from the life as a corporate executive to one as a corporate consultant and they continue be a constant source of inspiration and endearment. I also dedicate this book to the many corporate colleagues that I have associated with during my business and consulting career that proved many of the concepts presented in this work on a daily basis.

PROLOGUE

○ ○
"Our Life is what our thoughts make it"

—Marcus Aurelius

Sir Isaac Newton stands out in history as a leading scientist and many of his discoveries can be connected to numerous technologies and scientific tools being used in our modern world. Just a few examples are the Hubble Telescope, calculus, and spacecrafts being hurtled into space (White, 1997). It is a little known fact that Newton applied his scientific skills to many other areas of study including history, management, and organization principles.

It has been discovered that Newton prepared a study called History of the Church which was never published. His rough notes were sold at a Sotheby auction in 1936 and sections are scattered throughout Europe and Israel. He shared the belief of many scholars from the 17th century that most ancient civilizations were also the most knowledgeable and advanced.

He developed a chronology of the history of human civilization in a lengthy, loosely connected book that was eventually published after his death. During this study, he created methods of historical analysis similar to his approach to science which was to reduce everything to its simplest form.

In 1694, one of Newton's friends Charles Montagu was appointed Chancellor of the Exchequer. That year Newton was offered an appointment to be Master of the Royal Mint which he accepted. He had reached the conclusion that a unified explanation for all forces of nature was an impossible dream. Newton made a career change leaving academia, science, and historical research to become a general manager.

The staff at the Mint immediately observed Newton's management style which was very "hands on" and he launched a very careful analysis of all operating processes. His first goal was to increase efficiency and he utilized time-and-motion studies to determine where and how improvements could be implemented.

Several organization initiatives he implemented included:

- Established branch mints to decentralize operations.

- Instituted financial controls and a positive team approach of management.

- Demonstrated a high level of commitment and staff accountability for high quality results.

- Established clear goals to guide activities.

During his tenure, he was able to establish a highly productive operation where most inefficiency and corruption was eliminated.

This experience gave Newton an excellent opportunity to apply organization theory developed early in his scientific career. Newton and many others thought leaders from this era believed that major edifices constructed by ancient civilization were Earthly representations of the basic structure observed in the universe. Examples cited by White include stone circles found across Europe and the Pyramid at Giza (White, 1997). Newton took the position that these structures were a paradigm for the universe and an organizational pattern for future civilizations.

This study and the organizational theories derived clearly influenced his conceptualization of gravitation. He visualized parallels between the solar system and earthly systems. Newton's theory of gravitation was derived through a process of gradual awakening over a period of two decades. Very solid evidence has been documented that exploration of his various areas of interest led him to his theory of gravity.

It is at this point in history that modern science began which created the spark for the beginning of modern life (Berlinski, 1995). The universe is now viewed as highly organized and coordinated by mathematical laws. Newton's counterpart during this great period of awakening was Gottfried Leibnitz.

Leibnitz studied law, theology, math, history, geology, languages, biology, and manufacturing. He was a very social man who believed that universal methods could be employed to coordinate information and organize society and visualized computing machines, the concept of a formal system, a structure for DNA, and the future course of quantum mechanics. His quest was the explanation of the underlying connectivity of physical and social systems where universal laws exist that describe all primary forces of nature and, like Newton, mathematical formulas can be derived to define inner workings.

These are just two of the innumerable examples where profound thought leaders throughout history studied organization dynamics. Often submerged in the broader exploration of philosophy, astronomy, mathematics, history, biology, political science plus numerous other fields of focus, these dynamics were clearly articulated.

What follows is the exploration of earliest social units in prehistoric-society which provide a historical perspective of anthropological elements such as culture, leadership, communication techniques, division of labor, rules, decision-making and use of technology. Many early and modern anthropologists such as Mead, Durkheim, and Levi-Strauss provide a pragmatic view of studies of the basic inner workings of early human social units. From this beginning, pillars of modern organization theory and practice will be derived from the writings of early philosophers, social scientist, and students of management. Plato described the ideal structure for social organizations, including key components such as leadership, division of labor, training, authority and social unity. Rousseau examined the bond that creates unity in social units. Adam Smith formulated the framework for production in the early stages of the industrial revolution. Comte established Sociology as a way to discover general laws of social structure similar to those formulated in physics and biology. Max Weber defined bureaucracy and suggested it was the best administrative framework for the efficient pursuit of organizational goals. During this same period, Frederick Taylor modernized the principles of Adam Smith techniques for work flow analysis, job simplification, cost accounting, and time and motion study. Mayo and his colleagues linked worker productivity to the dynamics of group behavior.

These pillars of organization theory will be reexamined in the light of more recent experience and study, including the works of researchers and practitioners such as Herzberg, McGregor, Blake & Mouton, Bennis, Likert, Drucker, Crosby, Peters and Waterman, and most recently Hammer and Champy. They demonstrate a common theme which is geared toward organization effectiveness with particular emphasis on the organization and management of human resources. This examination can be further supported by very recent research and writings that focus on other fields of study such as the patterns of organization behavior that appear in nature plus the historical evolution of religion and warfare.

What has been most intriguing during the development of this work is the pragmatic application of these fundamental principles by several very successful corporate Chief Executives. They provided a prism that leads to the development of a current, easily applied theory with useable applications to improve organization effectiveness.

INTRODUCTION

o o o o o o o o o o o o o o o o o o o o o o o o o o o o o o o o o o o

"Wise men read very sharply all of your private history in your look and gait and behavior."

—Ralph Waldo Emerson

As managers and professionals we have been exposed to new organizational concepts over the last several years. Key organizational initiatives such as re-engineering, total customer satisfaction, CIP, TQM, employee empowerment, performance management and many others have been touted as the way out of the wilderness of organizational malaise and ineffectiveness. A decade or two ago, MBO, job enrichment, Theory Z, productivity improvement, new managerial grid, just to name a few were just as popular as many of the current organizational management theories. One of the most serious pitfalls that can affect implementation of many of these concepts, are situations where those leading the effort lack basic understanding of the fundamental organizational theory and principles involved. Many times programs are developed without a more in-depth knowledge or understanding of key underlying components that have been studied and applied over the last several hundred years. Too often specific applications will be viewed as a panacea (e.g., TQM) and those managing the endeavor lack this basic awareness. Examples of these principles are motivation, communications, leadership, group dynamics, feedback and organization commitment.

As a Business Executive and Corporate Consultant, my experience has been that, to a large extent, it is assumed these basics will happen as a natural course of events. Often times, many years have passed since

5

managers were exposed to formal education covering these topics or on some case never were taught the concepts. How often have you heard the comment "We recognize the need to communicate to our employees and I believe we're doing a credible job of getting current information out to everyone". Unfortunately, the employees are frustrated by the lack of information and rely heavily on the "organization grapevine". This lack of understanding often exists in similar fashion to many other facets of organizational structure and dynamics.

Organizations, as an entity, have existed since the beginning of human history. Archaeologists and anthropologists have studied and described these early organizational forms and early historians and philosophers developed theories and defined key components to explain organization dynamics. Out of these schools of thought evolved the field of social science which later led to the development of modern organization theory. Practitioners applying these theories include industrial engineers, industrial psychologist, operations research specialists, and organization development consultants.

A classic example of the damaging results when an organization functions ineffectively is a World War II disaster kept secret for fifty years. "A few weeks before D-Day, an exercise on the beaches in southern England ended abruptly with 946 men dead or missing and two troop carriers sunk. Through the combination of poor training, sloppy coordination and an almost complete failure of communication, Operation Tiger had become one of the greatest military disasters of World War II" (Sun Sentinel, April 24, 1994). Through the years, an untold number of other disasters have occurred in all segments of society because of the poor execution of these and many other basic organizational principles. It is my sincere desire that this work will shed light on these fundamental factors leading to organization success and bring into focus pragmatic, usable organization techniques that can guide managers and practitioners in their effort to build or improve organizational effectiveness. You will find that the presentation of this information is easily understood with limited usage of detailed philosophical or technical jargon.

It is through the knowledgeable application of the key principles involved that workable implementation of organizational theory and practices can be accomplished. Peter Drucker during a telecast presentation stressed that the term organization was unknown until 1950 and is just now beginning to be understood as an object of study. (George Washington U., May 3, 1994) Methods are now being developed to understand organization dynamics within the private, nonprofit and governmental market sectors. Performing in a modern organization is a new phenomenon and methodologies used to gain knowledge are just beginning to emerge. Fortunately, we have a rich history of social thought and scientific endeavor from which to draw.

1

PREHISTORIC ORGANIZATION

o o o o o o o o o o o o o o o o o o o o o o o o o o o o o o o
"Adapt or perish, now as ever, is natures inexorable imperative"

—H. G. Wells

Shortly after the dawn of mankind, humans began to ban together for survival and mutual benefit; thus, the first organizations were formed. One of the most illuminating descriptions of this early human existence was portrayed in the novel *The Clan of the Cave Bear* written by Jean M. Auel (Auel, 1989). She gathered extensive background information for her book from the works of many archaeologists and anthropologists to tell the story of prehistoric cave dwelling clan.

Dynamics described include leadership, communication, coordination, training, change, division of labor, decision-making, rules, environment, technology, and structure.

The clan was a small band of twenty nomads, which included men, women and children. The adults were four and one-half to five feet tall, large boned stocky and bow-legged walking upright on muscular legs and flat bare feet. Their arms were long in relation to the body with a large head resting on a short, thick neck. They traveled and lived together in a cave selected by one of the men who held the position as leader of the clan. They were a self-contained unit who gathered and hunted for food. Their method of communication was one-handed gestures and limited use of spoken words.

The common bond that united the clan was their combined totem which, in this case, was the cave bear viewed as supreme spirit and ultimate protector. The reverence toward their totem was the linking factor that unified the clan. Anthropologists studying the phenomenon defined this system of classification describing the relationship between man and nature as totemism where the totem can be a plant, animal or object and is the sacred symbol of the social group which binds them together with common purpose and culture. (Abercrombie, 1988)

The clan lived within the boundaries of changeless tradition where every facet of their life was determined by past events and norms of behavior based on their attempt to survive with a rigid resistance to change. They were extremely slow to adapt and discoveries were accidental and seldom utilized. Change required extreme effort and once adopted, the new way became as rigid as the old.

The leader always honored the totem and always insured that traditions of the clan were followed. This man was revered as a strong, fair and wise leader who exhibited hunting skills, instilled group confidence and was very even tempered. The leader of the Clan was the overseer of rules, rituals and was in control of all group decisions. There existed a very tight chain of command and a clear hierarchy with men in the dominant position, followed by women and children. One of the common rituals that occurred after the evening meal was the leader taking command of a ceremonial dance that included other men in the clan acting out the hunt for the meal. The bravery and hunting skills were demonstrated through the dance and the role of the leader as protector and provider was reinforced. The ritual demonstrated the hierarchical structure of authority with clearly defined areas of command and responsibility and a formal body of rules to govern the operation of this ancient social unit.

The main activity for men was hunting which supplied a major portion of food requirement for the clan and the sling was the primary weapon used to kill game. With muscular heavy-boned and bowed arms, they possessed precise manual dexterity and the great strength required to use the spear as a lance to be thrust at close range with tremendous force. The use of the spear and club required strength but learning to use a sling (a strip of flexible leather held together at both ends and whirled over the head to fling a round stone) took years of practice and concentration. There was tremendous prestige associated with the skillful use of this type of tool.

Usually, the women gathered food throughout the same area used to hunt and prepared most meals for the entire clan. They also collected firewood, tended to the needs of the young children and were expected to wait on the men. One woman held the position of medicine woman which required a high level of expertise and knowledge and late in life this duty was passed to a selected young female member of the clan. The women would also dig a cooking pit using pointed sticks as the tool to break the soil which was then placed in leather sacks and removed from the cooking area. A stone hand ax was used to chop large fallen logs so that they could be dragged to a woodpile near the cave. The division of labor for this primitive unit was well defined and primarily determined by clan tradition. The technical prowess exhibited through use of tools and application of knowledge by these early humans was critical to their survival and carefully passed from generation to generation.

Anthropology Forms Foundation

Many of the basic concepts being studied and discussed in relation to the formation of modern organizations were first defined by anthropologists and many of their discoveries were depicted in Jean Auel's book. Leaders in this branch of science have created the foundation of knowledge that other social scientist and organization theorists have incorporated very effectively into their fields of study. (Abercrombie, 1988)

One of the best known anthropologists is Margaret Mead who reported very solid evidence that culture shapes human habits and behavior. Similar to the culture observed in Clan of the Cave Bear, her studies demonstrated that the division of labor between men and women was based on social norms rather than biological roots. She was instrumental in clearly defining culture as the symbolic and learned non-biological aspects of human society including language, custom and convention that distinguishes human behavior. Cultural anthropologists have concluded that human behavior is largely culturally and not genetically determined, where a total set of beliefs, customs or way of life of particular social units establish belief systems, values and ideology.

One of the founding fathers of sociology, Emile Durheim, was greatly influenced by early philosophers and the study of primitive societies. He established the concept of the <u>Conscience Collective</u> which explained the solidarity of primitive societies based on common beliefs and consensus. It was his premise that individuals in organizations were molded and constrained by their social environment and he concluded that human behavior is influenced by the values of a social unit which have become internalized rather than acting as external constraints.

He also suggested that sacred objects symbolize the social unit and embodied the ideals of primitive societies. Ceremonies served to reinforce collective values and solidify unity among individuals. This process was very identifiable in primitive culture and through the reinforcement of these external social influences, general consensus concerning values and accepted behavior establishes social order. In addition, the division of labor that existed in primitive cultures did not reduce the conscience collective and reinforced consensus, promoting a high degree of social order.

Modern anthropologists have also provided a wealth of insight into the psychology of primitive societies. Claude Levi-Strauss studied the conceptual activities of primitive humans and concluded that culture shapes individual thought which drives the observable actions. The study of myths, which are narratives of the elders in primitive cultures, can explain their thought process to explain how they organize the relationship of power, submission, work, play, environment and social unity. These cultural manifestations can be observed in pairs demonstrating opposite attributes such as good and evil and viewed as a system of signs or a form of language. These social norms are learned and shape the thinking of individuals which can be observed as recurring patterns of social behavior.

One can observe consistent, organized and established relationships within a social unit in similar fashion to the study of other physical or biological systems. Studying early cultures as a system can create an insight into how these primitive social units are similar to modern organizations where this collection of interrelated parts can be observed as functioning whole that exists to achieve some purpose or goal.

The understanding of prehistoric social units provides an excellent foundation for further exploration of social theorists which began the progression toward the formation of early social and physical science. Early thought leaders began to articulate the social characteristics observed in society that anthropologists contend have existed since the beginning of human history. As we review this consistent pattern of social evolution, the fundamental nature of social behavior within the context of an organization becomes much clearer.

2

SOCIAL THEORY

"Man's greatness lies in his power of thought."

—Blaise Pascal

Most early social and scientific theory was developed by philosophers and many focused on the origin and structure of the universe and fundamental human nature. One of the earliest recorded theorists was Aristotle whose writings date back to 340 B.C. (Hawking, 1989). In Stephen Hawking's book, *A Brief History of Time*, he traces this early evolution of scientific theory describing the formation and structure of the universe which established the foundation for modern physics. Aristotle believed that the earth was stationary with all structures in the universe circulating around the earth which was supported by Ptolemy in the Second Century, A.D. This model, that included the earth as the center surrounded by eight spheres, was adopted by the Christian Church as the universe described in the Scriptures.

In 1514, Copernicus proposed a theory where the sun was the stationary center with the earth and planets moving in orbits around the sun. A century later this idea gained support when Galileo began observing the night sky with the newly invented telescope. In 1687, Newton developed the concept of gravity supported by mathematical calculations to explain the movement of bodies in the universe.

In addition to theories on the structure of the universe, many attempted to explain the origins of human civilization. St. Augustine proposed that society was evolving based on his interpretation of the Book of Genesis and the universe was created in 5000 B.C. Hawking indicates that his time of origin was amazingly close to 10,000 B.C. which is the date archaeologists have specified that civilization originated. Aristotle, along with most Greek philosophers, did not accept the creation theory and held to the belief that human civilization and the universe had always existed and would exist forever.

One of the most prominent Greek philosophers, Plato, founded the first university in the western world about 387 B.C. and the curriculum included science and philosophy (Kaplan, 1951). He was convinced that the salvation of society would be determined by the proper training of its potential leaders. His greatest work, *The Republic*, was the first utopia described in literature and formulated an ideal structure for social institutions and relationships including leadership, division of labor, training, social authority, social unity and values, and individual freedom. His writings influenced many philosophers and social scientists and established a model for the development of social theory. (e.g., Rousseau believed that he developed the best model for education in the world).

Plato believed that leaders must be philosophers who exhibit love of honor, wisdom, learning, truth, knowledge, sociable behavior, even tempered emotion and are actively involved in the environment around them. He believed that various types of workers were required for community success which included: farmers, builders, weavers, shoemakers, carpenters, merchants, and retailers. Even though he believed that men were superior to women he proposed that men and women should have equal access to all forms of labor. Critical social values were leadership wisdom, citizen temperance, social harmony and political equality. He emphasized the importance of agreement on common purpose by all members of an organization where differences are resolved, unity reigns, people are empowered with the freedom of an educated choice and responsibility is accepted for the results of actions. His theory of ideas was based on the belief that reality supersedes observable phenomenon and true philosophers have a vision of this reality.

The Age of Reason

In the late 1700's, Immanuel Kant supported a combined Greek and St. Augustine philosophical viewpoint. Also during this century, other philosophers and social theorists were beginning to theorize on the nature and structure of social organizations. Kant focused on this theological and early scientific argument by taking the position that these questions were contradictions of pure reason and that equally logical arguments could be made for both theories. Ironically, Levi Strauss, in his study of cognitive anthropology, described this phenomenon of opposing arguments as a fundamental characteristic exhibited by primitive humans and observed in prehistoric societies. Many social theorists began to develop the social sciences and physical scientists continued to argue to establish the correct theory to explain the formation of the universe. Hawking traces the evolution of these theories concerning the nature of the universe but more importantly, for purpose of this work, describes the essence of scientific theory. He stresses that a theory is a model of the subject being explained with a set of rules to measure the elements being observed. "It must accurately describe a large class of observations on the basis of the model that contains a few arbitrary elements, and it must make definite predictions about the results of future observations." (Hawking, 1988) An example he used was Newton's theory of gravity "in which bodies attracted each other with a force that was proportional to the square of the distance between them". Hawking's goal is to provide a single grand theory that explains the fundamental nature of the universe.

In a similar fashion, it is possible to trace the evolution of organization theory. In the early 18th Century, roughly fifty years prior to the writing of Immanuel Kant, a French social theorist, Charles Montesquieu, began to focus on the study of social science. His book, *The Spirit of the Laws*, published in 1748, outlined the relationship between religion, education, government and geography and his earlier writings described French society during this period. (Abercrombie, 1988) He also began to predict the long term viability of a society based on observable traits and analyzed the social causes of the success and failure of empires. His works influenced social science throughout the next century, and his concept 'separation of powers' is a fundamental principle of the U.S. Government. He theorized that any society that relies on forced compliance cannot survive.

Another philosopher that inspired the concept of freedom was Jean Jacques Rousseau who wrote about man, the human community and social order in *The Social Contract* published in 1762. He became an inspiration for political revolution and further defined key terms such as "right" "liberty", and "law". (Beardsley, 1960) He examined the true nature of the bond that creates unity in a social unit and how humans influence the society that surrounds them; thus, unknowingly becoming a pioneer social scientist. He defined the Social Contract as an alliance of individuals where "Each of us puts his person and all his power in common under the supreme direction of the general will, and, in our corporate capacity, we receive each member as an indivisible part of the whole". "This act of association creates a moral and collective body,…and receiving from this act its unity, its common identity, its life, and its will." (Beardsley, 1960) He painted a very optimistic picture of the ability of people in such an alliance to resolve differing opinions as long as the individuals receive necessary information and seriously deliberate together concerning these differences. It was his belief that under these circumstances the decision reached would always be good but when factions are formed and remain unresolved the common interest is lost. As long as individuals perceive themselves as a unified entity where they are concerned with their common survival and mutual well being, he believed, the alliance would prevail. With this climate of mutual trust the unit's common sense will insure that they act wisely, but when this unity fades that the seeds of destruction begin to take hold. This highly positive view of human nature puts great faith in the collective ability of a unified association but requires that individuals honestly state their views, propose solutions and be open to collective discussion. This clarification of universality in law laid the foundation for many of his successors such as Kant and many others.

Most organizations today can trace their roots back to the pin factory that Adam Smith described in *The Wealth of Nations* published in 1776. (Hammer & Champy, 1993) This philosopher and economist writing at the same time as Rousseau, focused much of his study on division of labor at this early period of the industrial revolution. Many American companies begin to utilize his organization principles to develop the vast majority of business processes. Smith wrote "The greatest improvement in the productive power of labor, and the greater part of the skill, dexterity, and judgement with which it is any where directed, or applied, seem to have been the effects of the division of labor." (Matteson, 1993) As was noted earlier, this was also a key dynamic studied by anthropologists researching primitive societies. In his work, Smith described how a pin-making production could be broken down into 18 distinct operations and contended that this system would greatly improve efficiency and requires a much lower worker skill level.

He believed that improved productivity was accomplished due to improved worker dexterity, reduced workflow time requirements and greater potential for use of machines to supplement labor. These simple principles could be applied to a wide variety of enterprises and would form the basis by which the business was organized and a process for developing the most effective structure.

Social Science Formalized

During the next century, several philosophers and social theorists began to promote sociology as the scientific study of social institutions and relationships. One of the founders of sociology in the late 18th Century, was a French aristocrat who was an officer in the French

Army and later conducted a number of educational experiments. Claude Saint-Simon influenced August Comte who has been recognized as the founder of sociology through his writings concerning the laws of social change and organization. He became a strong proponent for use of scientific principles to gain an understanding social evolution and led to theories developed by Comte, Spencer and Durkheim. Change was viewed as the adaptation of social systems to the environment which required a higher level of advancement at each successive stage of development. It was the growth of knowledge and increased environmental complexity that drove the need for progressive evolution to insure the survival of a social organization. This organic analogy became a reoccurring theme in later writings and study.

The origination of the concept of sociology as a scientific discipline was put forth by Auguste Comte in his book, *Systeme de Politique Positive*, published in 1850. (Beardsley, 1960) He viewed it as a science utilizing key principles such as observation, experimenting, and evaluation and focused a large degree of his research on the study of division of labor. He believed that social scientist would discover general laws of social structure similar to those found in physics and biology. (Abercrombie, 1988)

In the English version of his book translated by J.H. Bridges, 1865, Comte's descriptions of the principles of this new science were outlined. He believed that the foundations for sociology originated in mathematics and astronomy, which led to the study of physics and biology. The study of social phenomenon was a logical extension of these basic sciences and would utilize the same systematic techniques. He acknowledged that only a few theorists had accepted his principle laws of sociology; however, that did not discourage further development of the science.

One of his original concepts was the general law of human development. This law specifies that all human societies pass through three stages beginning with imagination requiring no proof, followed by discussion, which define abstractions, and finally demonstration requiring a specific view of facts. All scientific thought and social dynamics were purported to pass through these phases of development in succession and establishing the foundation of social science and became known as the Evolutionary Theory. (Abercrombie, 1988) He theorized that all social entities inevitably pass through these stages of development and viewed evolution as the growth of functional specialization of structures and the better adaptation of parts. The historical analogy used was the division of history into ancient, medieval and modern.

Comte believed that use of scientific methodology to evaluate theories without the goal of bettering humanity was highly irrational and that sociology must be included with other hard sciences such as physics to achieve this aim. Through the scientific study of society, the understanding of a complete system of human life would be possible. He observed that biologist viewed sociology as extension of their laws and tended to explain sociological facts on the basis of climate and race which he contends were secondary to the laws of sociology. Thus, true understanding of social dynamics would result from the systematic identification of these social variables and scientific testing of observed actives.

Mankind had been struggling to understand the organization of social existence which Comte believed had been impossible up to the time that the science of sociology was formed based on the law of historical development. With this scientific study of human society two primary social forces could be explained which are the affect of social organization on the world and the binding together of component parts. Comte stressed that social units function based on the actions of individual members and "efficiency of these members depends on their working in cooperation, whether instinctively or with design". (Beardsley, 1960) This external force influences the behavior of individuals and links the elements of the unit. Clearly, he established the discipline which formulated a methodology to study and explain how social units function.

3

DAWN OF THE 20TH CENTURY

o o o o o o o o o o o o o o o o o o o o o o o o o o o o o o
"When a thing is done, it's done. Don't look back. Look forward to the next objective."

—*George C. Marshall*

The social scientist that created the bridge between the social theories of the 19th century and early 20th century organization theory is Max Weber. He was a prolific writer, born and educated in Germany, who had great insight into the workings of modern industrial society and was viewed as the founder of modern sociology. In addition to establishing guidelines for sociological study and the exploration of Western society, he developed concrete theories concerning leadership and the value of a beauracratic organization structure. His book *The Theory of Social and Economic Organizations* highlights many of these principles (Weber, 1964). Bureaucracy could provide efficiency and predictability to administrative operations of an organization similar to the concepts Frederick Taylor proposed for production operations.

Weber outlined a number of critical characteristics of this type of organization structure that could be applied to all enterprises serving the ideal of achieving goals. They include formal position responsibilities, clearly defined hierarchy, position descriptions, selection based on technical capability, formal salary guidelines, professional commitment, and code of organization conduct. He further traced the history of this type of organization as demonstrated in hospitals, organized religion, large scale corporate enterprises, and the military. As society has evolved, the importance of technical qualifications in the organization continues to increase along with specialized knowledge and authority becomes concentrated at one single position. Weber became a strong proponent of the bureaucratic organization based on his assessment that it provided the highest level of efficiency and the most logical method of controlling human behavior. He believed it was the most stable, disciplined and reliable form of organization and could be applied to all types of administrative requirements. This organization structure and process became indispensable when meeting most administrative needs of modern society. This control is based on technical and organizational knowledge which led to his prediction that most of capitalistic society would be organized into large scale corporate groups as a result of the dominance of precision machinery in the mass production of goods. History has shown that this structural form has dominated most public and private organizations during the latter part of this century. In addition, he characterized authority as legal-rational, traditional or charismatic and specified that legal-rational authority is prevalent within a bureaucratic organization structure. Authority is defined as the exercise of power where people willingly follow direction because they recognize this use of power as legitimate. (Abercrombie, 1988). Traditional authority is prevalent in less advanced societies where acceptance of power is based on traditional and long standing practice. In those circumstances where commands are obeyed because individuals believe in the extraordinary characteristics of their leader, charismatic authority is the basis of power. In all cases, Weber concluded that the power must have some basis of legitimacy and the leadership of the organization usually exercises some control over members or participants.

Unfortunately, he died suddenly of pneumonia in 1920 at the height of his intellectual capability. His work in articulating organizational structure and leadership is highly relevant in the study of modern organization theory and his legacy remains.

Max Weber acknowledged that Frederick Taylor was a pioneer in the development of methods for the rational organization of work in large scale business firms.

> "Practice, and the resulting skill, can only be perfected by rational and continuous specialization. Today, it is worked out on a basis which is largely empirical, guided by considerations of minimizing costs in the interest of profitability, and limited by these interests." (Weber, 1964, Page 261)

This Taylor system, as Weber called it, was very compatible with his bureaucratic structure and could lead to the formulation of a rational, planned economy. Thus, the scientific management methodology also began to develop during this period of the early 20th century. Frederick Taylor was the most prominent architect of this movement focused on changing the management of business to a much greater emphasis on increased profit. (Abercrombie, 1988)

There are several key components to the Taylor system that would lead to increased work force efficiency. It was his contention that the production process could be analyzed systematically and organized into component parts. Each workers position was to be simplified and wherever possible refined to a limited task. Through this simplification, efficiency would be enhanced because the skill required for each job was greatly reduced which leads to cheaper costs of labor. This more technically devised division of labor removed control from the first line production operation placing it with a new breed of management specialists that had the maximization of profit as their primary mission.

Professional managers now would have full control of the work place to insure maximum efficiency. They were also responsible for the coordination of all production operations which became much more critical due to the increased specialization and differentiation of work.

The goal to reduce the skill requirements of workers greatly increased the challenge for the manager to orchestrate the production process. The primary tool that was introduced to aid managers in their new role was systematic time-and-motion study which formed the foundation for manufacturing cost accounting. Each step in the process could be reduced to the simplest task and a very precise cost associated with each of these jobs. The stop watch became indispensable for the legions of industrial engineers and cost accountants that measured and controlled the output required.

One little known fact of the Taylor system was his proposed reward system which provided employees with the opportunity to share in the profit improvement. The same tools used to impact the profitability of the enterprise could be used to design compensation practices so that worker pay is based on their efforts which resulted in increased profit. One of the few early applications of this concept was the Scanlon Plan. Ironically, there has been expanded use of this approach over the last several years in the form of Gain Sharing and Employee Stock Ownership Plans even though this was a seldom used element of the Taylor system.

Scientific Management established a framework for the organization of work throughout the 20th century which led to reduce the skill requirements for first line workers and established the role of management within a modern industrial organization.

The shift of this function from the sole control of the owners to an enterprise led by managers who develop more highly specialized skills for professional management became a predominant feature within industry. This movement has been directly linked to the manufacturing technology utilized by the auto industry at the beginning of the century in the form of the first assembly lines. It was Taylor's basic work flow design that created the structure for an efficient assembly operation. This technology has continued to evolve through the century yet the fundamental principles remain unchanged which include work simplification, continuous improvement of efficiency, and the capture of critical management information.

As one views modern industry, it becomes obvious that the concepts put forth by Taylor and Weber dominated the structure and work processes that existed throughout the 20th Century. Most of us have been exposed to a variety of organizational settings while growing up and during our careers. To a large extent the structure has been bureaucratic with defined operating systems. During the latter portion of the 20th century, this basic model became second nature and was often applied without analysis or evaluation of other approaches. The model evolved over the years with most managers and practitioners utilizing a very traditional structure that has was generally accepted and familiar.

Up to this point, little concern was being shown in this efficiency paradigm for the needs of workers and the level of understanding of this phenomenon was minimal. The Hawthorne Study became a landmark research effort that began to shift the focus from mechanistic results to a better understanding organization dynamics. The study was conducted at a Western Electric manufacturing plant in 1927 and designed to determine the effect of lighting on worker productivity. The initial results proved to be inconclusive which triggered the hypothesis that the workers being studied were reacting psychologically rather than physiologically and led to further study to better understand the workers. (Matteson, 1993)

This additional research was conducted in a special testing area and small group of women were selected to be the subjects of the study. The area was a replica of the production operation and each participant was individually briefed on the details of the experiment. They were prepared for the evaluation of the study and told to work at a relaxed pace. This high level of communication was continued and the women were updated as the project plans changed. Their input was solicited and methods that were not approved by the group were excluded from the study.

The research was carefully structured to determine the effects of a variety of working conditions on the output of the group (e.g., pay, breaks, work schedule) as the study continued, the variables were changed to identify which conditions had the greatest impact on results. It became increasingly evident that the workers were reacting to some other phenomenon than the conditions applied because the output continued to improve in a steady upward direction as the experiment progressed. Based on current knowledge, it is obvious that the high level of communications, lack of close supervisory monitoring, special recognition, and continuous feedback of results had a very positive influence on the women. They truly enjoyed the general environment and the leadership style being utilized matched their effectiveness level. The women knew that company management was very interested in them and they were all part of a very important project.

One of the most striking observations was the group dynamics that evolved during the study. Certain members of the group assumed a strong leadership role and the participants were clearly focused on their primary mission to continuously improve the production level. The researchers reached the conclusion that the results were not caused by changed working conditions but could be linked to positive group cohesion and commitment to the primary group mission.

When the results were further evaluated and publicized, it became a "watershed" event in the evolution of organization dynamics. It generated a long line of research and writings focused on the critical nature of the human element versus structural influence. It was the beginning of the modern exploration into the key elements of human resources management as they relate to the overall effectiveness of social units. Many leaders, writers, and scientists recognized the importance of the human element in the creation of organization effectiveness. Mankind was able to transport large groups across great distances, build complicated and awe inspiring structures, establish thriving economic enterprises, design utopian societies, and this ability to organize activities insured the survival of ancient clans in spite of limited resources and an extremely hostile environment. It is from this foundation that numerous researchers and practitioners have continued the quest to understand organization dynamics and improved effectiveness.

4

THE MODERN ORGANIZATION

During the 1950's, the social science and management science perspective began to merge and the importance of the human element in the equation leading to organization effectiveness began to emerge. The individual player was no longer just an insignificant element in the mechanistic organization structure designed to direct behavior but a critical force leading to organizational success. It was now becoming important that organization dynamics be effectively developed and utilized to begin to truly tap the power of human resources and counteract negative consequences such as turnover, sabotage, poor quality, and low morale. Efforts were beginning to be channeled toward mutually accepted goals and workers were asked to make use of their minds in concert with their bodies.

One of the most widely read and quoted theorists during this era is Douglas McGregor and his article "The Human Side of Enterprise" (1957) successfully merged the understanding of the social science with the practice of industrial management. With his combined perspective as philosopher, educator, and manager, he formulated his theory of organization management. (Matteson, 1993) He created a vision where creative human energy becomes available within an organization when perceptive imagination is applied to understand the organization of human effort.

McGregor believed that people want to contribute to their organization and proposed two different assumptions about individual motivation. The first, he labeled "Theory X" where people are viewed lazy and indifferent to work, require constant direction, want to avoid responsibility, and lack ambition. Because of this lack of commitment, they must be coerced, controlled or even threatened with punishment to get results. The other, "Theory Y" has a much more positive view of human nature and assumes that work can be satisfying. People will direct themselves toward the pursuit of organizational objectives and have the capacity to seek as well as accept responsibility. Organizational activity can be as natural as play and individuals are capable of applying imagination, ingenuity, and creativity to achieve results.

He recommends the use of what Peter Drucker called "management by objectives" rather than "management by control" and encouraged the effective application of organization dynamics (e.g., proactive leadership and standards of performance). He proposed that managers move away from the conventional organizational theory which was applied through the bureaucratic structure and scientific management practices. It was time to move away from a dynamics designed to control people as if they were children toward those which allow adult self-motivation.

As we have seen, the prehistoric clan was highly self-sufficient and capable of not only surviving but thriving under very hostile conditions. Many early philosophers and social theorists have a very enlightened view of human nature. Plato encouraged comprehensive education and Rousseau had utmost confidence that humans provided with valid information could reach sound decisions concerning necessary social action. In spite of this profound view, management gravitated in the direction of tight control and the bureaucratic organization structure espoused by Weber and Taylor.

McGregor encouraged organization practitioners to apply Theory Y on a slow progressive basis and focus on several key organization dynamics. A delegating leadership style was recommended where organization members are empowered to direct their own activities and assume responsibility for personal results. Sears was identified as a company that had decentralized control with a much flatter organization structure. The division of labor shifted from narrowly focused duties to enlarged job responsibilities where greater use of the mind was involved. Participative decision making could be utilized to allow individuals to share in the shaping of the enterprises direction.

At the same time GE and General Mills were experimenting with the use of MBO where subordinates were encouraged to take greater responsibility for eliciting performance feedback while playing a much larger role in planning and managing their activities. McGregor painted a picture where the same ingenuity that changed technological ideas into realities could be applied to the human side of enterprise to gain even greater organization effectiveness.

New Model Emerges

Peter Drucker has been one of the premier developers of management as an established profession. It was Weber who defined the critical role of management in the modern organization and Drucker became one of the most widely studied educators to operationalize the function. He determined that one of the most vital roles of management was the development and implementation of an organization planning process. He was a strong advocate of a delegating leadership style where planning and decision making is decentralized. This type of organization requires that the entire organization have complete awareness of the mission, goals, and measures of success for their endeavors. The key tool utilized to accomplish this is a long range plan that involves most of the organization and provides focus for coordinated direction.

One of his more recent books that applies many of his earlier concepts is **Innovation and Entrepreneurship** (Drucker, 1985) which highlights many of the key attributes of an entrepreneurial organization. To begin, the primary organization leaders should evaluate the external environment to determine the viability of current organization practices. Within this context, internal processes need to be analyzed to determine effectiveness and identify new ventures. For a business enterprise this would include market analysis, distribution channels, products, technologies, and methods of operation. The analysis must be an honest and penetrating appraisal that provides information from which leaders can formulate long range strategic direction. Included in the analysis are clear measurable indicators of success which may be used to formulate targeted goals and evaluate results. Once the road map has been established, a well coordinated operating plan can be developed which includes objectives, budgets, and individual accountability.

This planning process becomes the key ingredient that allows greater decentralization and reliance on individual accountability. Organization leaders in conjunction with their work unit develop measurable objectives where each individual develops specific objectives that support group objectives. This is accomplished after the overall mission has been clearly communicated throughout the organization and specific areas of focus have been identified. Work unit managers finalize action plans with individual contributors and work unit plans are rolled together into a cohesive organization operating plan. One of the most critical elements of this process is the establishment of review check points during the planning cycle where individuals report results compared to plan to their management who summarize progress for senior management. It must be viewed as a dynamic plan with guidelines for adjusting expectation based on environmental or organizational changes. To the greatest extent possible, each member of the organization plans and controls the results for their area of responsibility while senior executives further develop and refine long term strategy to insure that required assignments are accomplished in a well coordinated fashion.

As these concepts began to be applied, it was becoming very evident that historical concepts of worker motivation were being dramatically altered. It was Frederick Herzberg who stressed the need for organization leaders to shift their focus from structural factors such as environment and working conditions to the design of work itself. His theories created a tremendous amount of controversy. At the foundation of his research was the belief that many organization dynamics such as leadership, group activity, and organization structure can be channeled to improve human relations, organization efficiency, and worker satisfaction.

In much of his work, Frederick Herzberg theorized that work or skill development is a much more powerful motivator than factors such as organization administration, working conditions, and salary. (Matteson, 1993) He continued to stress the need to study how work is distributed and structured rather than a continuing overemphasis on surrounding conditions. Satisfying the human desire to grow and achieve is a great underutilized motivator and by structuring work activity to unleash this potential greatly improves organization results.

The most significant organization applications developed from Herzberg's theory of motivation was job enrichment. This approach to job design was a major shift from the work simplification methodology practiced by proponents of Scientific Management. Rather than highly specialized and routine job duties, increased skill requirements and greater responsibility for planning and control are included in the enriched job. This tended to have an upward ripple affect on the organizations that implemented this approach and individual contributors assumed many traditional management responsibilities which resulted in the management of their own work. With this greater involvement in the total realm of the individual job responsibility, the person's work could become the primary motivational force within an organization. The modern term for job enrichment is employee empowerment where individual ability to perform a variety of skills and responsibilities that increase autonomy and discretion in the areas such as problem solving, scheduling, quality, and working procedures are encouraged.

The ingredients he prescribed to better utilize critical organization dynamics include a culture that supports individual responsibility and creativity, division of labor which provides greater span of control at all levels, human motivation based on job satisfaction, and a flexible structure that is built around achievement needs of people. His research, writings, and promotion of these concepts had a tremendous impact on organization theory and applications lasting well into the 1970's.

Best known for his depiction of the role managers play in linking organization units, Rensis Likert formulated organization methods designed to maximize coordinated, cooperative efforts directed toward accomplishing organization goals. He detailed the critical concepts involved in *New Patterns of Management* (Cummings, 1969) which would lead to effective organization management.

Most importantly, he contends that individual workers need to perceive that they may achieve a personally satisfying work life while they receive equitable and reliable economic rewards. This link between full use of abilities and financial success needs to exist at all organizational levels rather than restricting such success exclusively to the uppermost level. Organizations that encourage people to develop their competencies and demonstrate how they impact organization results will achieve high levels of productivity and worker motivation.

In addition, this high level of cooperative motivation should also be supported by a management leadership style that builds and maintains a personal sense of self worth and importance. Individuals throughout the organization should view interactions between members as positive and supportive. This results in an organization climate which promotes and reinforces cooperation and team unity where the environment is much more than surface behavior and exists based on a sense of common values, expectations and desire for mutually beneficial results.

The building blocks for this effective and efficient organization are well developed and coordinated work teams which have a sense of group involvement and loyalty. Team members are involved in the work of one or more units that have reasonable stable membership with a sense of group loyalty. Team leaders serve as "linking pins" where they have shared membership between their management team and the organization unit they lead. Key responsibilities include communications, planning, conflict resolution, and reinforcement of organization cohesiveness and each leader shares in the work of both groups. Ideally, each unit understands how their results contribute to the achievement of total enterprise goals while experiencing the esprit de corp of their personal teams.

Likert stressed that the goal setting process espoused by Drucker should be an ongoing process which includes the active involvement of all work groups. Utilizing the primary organization goals developed by senior management as a guide, detailed individual and work unit objectives are established in a challenging yet realistic manner that are designed to accomplish the higher level goals. To the highest degree possible, each member of the enterprise is involved in the decision making process involved in the development of these operating plans. His experience suggested that this approach would result in cooperative motivation among workers, coordination within and between organization work units and development of stretch goals throughout the organization.

When applying these principles, he concluded that it was critical that management take into account the unique culture of the enterprise. Success depends on development of the human interaction skills of supervisors and managers including team leadership and knowledge of group dynamics. This skill building in conjunction with the reinforcement of supportive relationships through effective tailoring of compensation systems, decision making methods, and organization communications were critical to effective management of the organization. To maintain or improve this effectiveness, he recommended that the assessment of the organization of human activity accompanied by corrective action where applicable should be continuous.

He conducted numerous research projects which examined the effect of organization management style on enterprise productivity improvement. It was clearly demonstrated that short term crash programs where management applied high levels of direct hierarchical pressure were self-defeating. By tracking several critical productivity measures such as cost and output, he found that a longer range approach where his principles were consistently applied achieved the highest productivity and superior long term performance and the crash effort brought poor results.

One of Likert's greatest contributions was the development of organization measures which identify future problem areas that can be used to develop corrective action which can greatly improve organization results. Most commonly used performance measures such as financial data look back and problems often reach critical proportions before being recognized. He demonstrated that data focused on the human aspects of the enterprise may be analyzed and problem areas can be identified one or more years prior to reaching a serious level. By simply measuring the implementation level of each key management principle, organization leaders can determine the extent that they are able to achieve critical goals fully and efficiently. He demonstrated that continuous measurement and analysis of primary human factors can identify trends which can prevent costly long range consequences of deteriorating organization effectiveness.

Organization Development

During this era a wide variety of researchers and practitioners discussed, proposed, and implemented numerous strategies that incorporated principles that better utilized and met the motivational needs of human resources plus Organization Development began to emerge as a profession with mixed results. Programs that placed excessive emphasis on the human element gained limited measurable results while productivity improvement specialists utilizing scientific management techniques gained popularity. Two industrial psychologists that successfully operationalized the dual focus on the concern for production and the needs of people were Robert Blake and Jane Mouton. They developed an organization model which incorporated many of the theories and methods of the individuals reviewed thus far plus numerous others. They synthesized much of the research and writings from the fields of organization behavior, business administration, political science, industrial psychology, psychiatry, and education into a system described as a Managerial Grid.

They identified three primary organizational concerns as achievement of tangible results (production), involvement of subordinates and colleagues within an organization as distinctive individuals (people), and use of hierarchy to achieve productivity with and through people that mesh and are represented graphically in a two dimensional grid. They describe these elements and provide a methodology for successful implementation of a system designed to mobilize human efforts so that organizations can maximize performance in their widely read book *The New Managerial Grid* (1978).

New insights into leader/organization member behavior with their effects upon organization and individual effectiveness and a diagnostic method designed to assess leadership style were outlined by the authors in great detail. The grid system highlights for organization leaders methods for managing conflict, accelerating learning from group experience, and utilizing teamwork to enhance problem solving and decision making.

Based on their research, they concluded that the leadership style which places a high degree of emphasis on organization productivity coupled with a sincere concern for the well being of people will gain results from people who are committed to a "common stake" in organization purpose and lead to relationships of trust and respect within the social unit. Leaders who focus primarily on productivity or people needs will either gain efficiency through obedience and coercion or less than optimum effectiveness in a comfortable environment. The least effective style is where the leader exerts the minimum effort required to obtain results and demonstrates the level of concern that will ensure survival within an organization. At the center of the grid is the style which elicits adequate performance by balancing work requirements with the need to maintain a satisfactory level of morale.

Organization leadership that presumes an inherent link between productivity requirements and the needs of people for full and meaningful work experiences will lead to standards of excellence and achievement of optimum results. Implementation of these values involves the utilization of several key organizational characteristics. The planning process includes individuals at all levels in the review of relevant success factors and the establishment of goals to reach desired mutual outcomes. Roles are clearly defined within the framework of the whole with established procedures and ground rules. There is consistent feedback on progress where leaders assist in removal of roadblocks and there is agreement on revision of critical goals. The evaluation process is continuous with an emphasis on experiential learning and long term improvement. To the highest degree possible, work requirements are matched with individual capabilities and developmental needs when determining necessary division of labor.

They concluded that there should be a constant focus on creating an organization environment where leaders and individual contributors understand critical issues and have a combined stake in most outcomes. Within the context of widespread commitment to organization goals and operational efficiency/profitability, leaders effectively promote teamwork. Individuals who share responsibility for results pool information, review alternatives through shared thinking, and reach agreed upon solutions. This team approach achieves a high degree of team commitment and greatly facilitates implementation of action plans.

One of the most effective aspects of the Blake and Mouton system is a methodology for changing the organization culture which they define as traditions, precedents, and past practices that often control individual actions rather than the situational requirements or personal inclinations. What may result is an operating style centered in the past but poorly adapted to future requirements where leaders often lack understanding of the power of culture and the tremendous potential for cultural change. Relying on these traditional organizational methods, they would find, usually failed to bring about required operational results. This awareness of cultural influence developed during the 1970's along with the understanding that it was usually outside the influence of direct management control. When organization "buy in" was lacking, change efforts would have little chance for success.

Their recommended change model begins with a general orientation for key members on applied behavior science followed by an in-depth review of the Grid System with a few selected members of the organization. The next phase involves a detailed briefing of top management on the complete Grid OD process which sets the stage for pilot Grid System seminars in designated areas of the organization. The next suggested step is to conduct Pilot Teamwork Development with the top leaders to demonstrate how the system can be applied to build team effectiveness and develop a strategy to expand the effort throughout the organization. With this plan, new leadership approaches can be implemented which will survive the negative pressures that would most likely sabotage the change process.

The well documented results of the Grid System include development of mature organization relationships and increased productivity. The authors contend that the 9,9 orientation can provide the key to strengthening the free enterprise system and the political democracy foundation on which it rests.

An individual who formalized "organization development" as a specialized area of expertise is Warren Bennis who has written extensively, held significant organization leadership positions, and conducted numerous research efforts focused on organization effectiveness. He clearly established the study and enhancement of organization results as a recognized profession and greatly advanced the understanding of contemporary organization dynamics. (Cummings, 1969)

One of his dominant themes during the 60's and early 70's was the demise of the bureaucratic organization structure due to the conditions of the modern industrialized world. (Matteson, 1993) He described the bureaucratic structure as a useful social invention which evolved during the Industrial Revolution to organize the activities of a business enterprise. The key components include a clear chain of command, well defined organization procedures, organization progression based on technical competence, and formalized human interaction.

Bennis highlighted four critical social conditions that were clearly emerging during this era which tend to be even more pronounced today. First is very rapid and less predictable change which puts tremendous stress on the rules and rigidity of a bureaucratic structure. Second, the growth in size of modern organizations has outstripped the effectiveness of tight controls and administrative overhead. The third condition is the tremendous complexity of modern technology which breaks down the old trend where workers have narrowly structured responsibilities. The final and much more subtle factor is a change in the organization principles underlying management behavior. He points to many of the concepts stressed by behavioral scientists such as Douglas McGregor and Rensis Likert who illuminated the higher level needs of individuals, the need for more sharing of organization power, and increased emphasis on democratic ideas.

He predicted that future organizations would be organic rather than mechanical and would evolve in response to real time issues rather than programmed based on role expectations. The structure would consist of multi-disciplined project groups rather than stratified functional groups that are in constant state of flux to meet changing organization requirements. In this type of organization, individuals would learn to live with high levels of ambiguity, identify with this adaptive process, and be self directed. With this operating style, social structures lose the tendency to constrict behavior and increasingly promote creativity and thought.

Ironically, a series of social and economic events became the catalyst which initiated full scale applications of many of these organization concepts in the US and numerous other industrialized nations.

5

THE MODERN ERA

○ ○
"He is a rich man who can avail himself of all men's faculties."

—Emerson

During the 1970's the faith in the ability for US enterprise to dominate in a global economy was shaken dramatically. Japanese companies were highly successful in capturing major portions of the market world wide. Our leadership role was eroding badly and many companies were searching for methods to better structure and manage organizations. During the late 70's a pair of consultants from McKinsey & Company, Thomas Peters and Robert Waterman, completed a study of 75 companies that cut across most industries which they categorized as "Americas Best-Run Companies".

The result of this research was their book *In Search of Excellence* (1982) which burst upon the scene in the early 80's and was widely discussed throughout business, education, and media circles. The concepts and practices discussed were viewed by many as both proof and a methodology which could stem the tide and return US organizations to their rightful position of economic dominance. Several of the practices have been accepted and applied as sound principles for effective organization leadership and continue to be utilized as important management tools. One of the most notable examples is their description of a major tenet utilized by Hewlett Packard titled MBWA ("Management By Wandering Around") which is still recognized as a highly desirable management attribute and has become a fixture in many organizations.

During this period, several other books achieved similar success and recognition thus moving the study of organizations into the popular media from the academic and philosophical areas of study which were dominant throughout history. Thomas Peters and Robert Waterman started this trend with their work by identifying several characteristics which differentiated excellent, innovative companies.

First, there was an organizational tendency to get things done where leaders encourage their staff to rapidly try new ideas. When a problem or issue needed to be resolved, a small team would be formed to brainstorm the solution and implement required action. The product development process discovered was a small team approach with a mission to rapidly test new concepts with customers using a relatively inexpensive prototype. What stood out most was the high level of flexibility and mobility that permeated the organization and the consistent goal to counteract bureaucratic atrophy that usually occurs with organization growth. These organizations also developed a partnership relationship with their customers and constantly learned from those they support. Each insured an exceptional level of product quality, service, and reliability with the ability to clearly differentiate their capability from most of their competition. These innovators got a large portion of their new ideas from customers by listening very carefully on a continuous basis.

These creative organizations encouraged autonomy and entrepreneurship with numerous innovators at all levels where inventors populated a loose network of laboratories and let their imagination soar. Senior leaders encouraged and supported creative risk taking and allowed tremendous latitude. Productivity was gained through people where everyone has a mission to constantly improve quality and operating results. There was an effort not to over rely on capital investment or establish barriers between organization levels in an environment where each individual was viewed as a potential source for new ideas that could contribute to the continuous improvement process.

It was also found that the operating philosophy of the organization had much more impact on results than technology, resources, structure, innovation or timing. Senior management relied on the practice of involvement at the grass roots level and would often walk the plant floors or visit field locations. In most cases, these organizations had well defined and fully communicated values as guides for behavior. The organization charter was clearly established with constant focus on prioritized goals and the top performing companies appeared to remain focused on the business or markets they knew best.

Consistent with many of these attributes was the tendency for most companies to keep organization structure and systems very simple plus senior staff levels were extremely lean. They found that it was very common to have a corporate staff of less than 100 people running a multi-billion-dollar company. None were using the complex matrix structure that required multiple reporting relationships which had become very popular in the 60's and 70's and those that had tried this approach moved to much simpler structures. This study group emphasized autonomy for individual work groups while maintaining clear focus on key corporate values. 3M was recognized for organized chaos around product champions and DEC for total commitment to product reliability in an environment with blurred lines of authority.

The authors highlighted what appeared to be a dawning of a new age where organizations live their commitment to people and preference for action. They found that most of these key characteristics identified existed in the companies highlighted and were conspicuously absent in most large companies where managers had lost perspective on organization basics (e.g., quick action, customer service, practical innovation). American companies were floundering because of top heavy staff and cumbersome structures and systems. In contrast, excellent organizations appeared to have developed cultures which apply the values and methods of great leaders where the primary role of the chief executive is to champion the values of the enterprise.

TQM

One of the primary reasons recognized during this era for organization ineffectiveness was the lack of attention and emphasis by key members on high quality results. Japanese products and services which historically were noted for shoddy workmanship became the standard bearer for exceptional quality while many other nations including the US were struggling in this arena. Philip Crosby became a leader in a new service industry that became known as TQM (Total Quality Management) which set out to help organizations improve their effectiveness. In his book *Quality Is Free*, (1979) he demonstrated simple principles that could be used as a "road map" to improve organization results.

Using these principles and actual case histories, he described how effective TQM programs work and highlighted critical tools that maximize results. He developed a Quality Management Maturity Grid which describes and measures current status of any quality system and future evolutionary stages for a well developed program. He outlined a tested 14 step procedure that could be utilized by leaders to move an organization in the proper direction. A Make Certain Program was described which included a defect prevention methodology for administrative and non-production staff. Also included was a Management Style Evaluation which demonstrated how operating style can influence product quality.

Crosby found that the folklore of organization management stated that those with proper intentions will produce quality results. He stressed that quality management had become too critical to leave to chance because of tremendous increases in the cost of doing business and the cost savings associated with doing jobs right the first time may be one of the last opportunities to make profits controllable. Using his Quality Management Maturity Grid most leaders who have ultimate responsibility for the implementation of TQM as a long term strategic process, were provided a methodology to evaluate the effectiveness of quality efforts by simply gaining awareness of what is happening in the organization.

The Grid is divided into five stages of evolution and six critical organization measurement factors which describe various gradations within most operations in stages of development or deterioration based on commonly recognized organizational behaviors. Management understanding and attitude ranges from no comprehension of quality as a management tool to a goal where quality management becomes an essential part of an organization system. Quality organization status grows from being hidden in a key line function to the Quality Manager reporting to the CEO where prevention is the primary charter for the function. The goal for problem handling becomes, with only rare exceptions, an environment where most problems are prevented rather than one where they are handled on a reactive basis and organization infighting prevails. The Cost of quality as a % of sales improves from being totally unknown to being measured at roughly 20% and improved to a target of 2.5%. Quality improvement initiatives evolve from no structured activities to a goal of continuous improvement. The Strategy for the organization quality initiative becomes knowing why few quality problem exist versus no knowledge why problems exist.

The following is Crosby's 14 step process which could then be utilized as a road map to guide the organization to the optimum Quality Management Maturity level. Step One: Management of the organization must understand that improvement is required and clearly communicate their commitment to product or service defect prevention. This commitment is formalized as one of the critical organization policies and is consistently reinforced through decisions and operating actions.

Step Two: A cross functional Quality Improvement Team is established the function on a part time basis as overseers of the quality improvement program with responsibilities for improvement strategy development, department representation on the team, team representation to the department, leading department quality initiatives, and implementation of the improvement activity. The team mission is to develop a strategy and gain executive staff support for implementation of a detailed action plan which is closely monitored for results.

Step Three/Four: Specific quality measurement data is developed for each operating area and the cost of quality defects should be clearly communicated throughout the organization. It is critical that the information captured is easily understood and useable (e.g., defects per unit, percent defective). Also, the problems need to be classified based on seriousness, cause, and responsibility. This data can then be used to calculate the cost of poor quality in each key area of the enterprise with allowable bench marks for effective operation. One obvious category is the value of product sold returned by the customer for not meeting performance requirements and the cost of replacement, repair, or service. This methodology identifies high priority problems and suggests probable corrective action.

Step Five: Methods are developed to raise the concern for all members of an organization to a high level of commitment to exceptional quality results. The essential ingredients are regular meeting between management and staff to review specific problems and develop improvement action plans. Quality results need to be communicated in a clear and consistent fashion utilizing highly visible and various methods such as posters, newsletters, and special events. An environment that stresses continuous improvement toward stretch goals is developed and maintained.

Step Six: Corrective Action is taken based on issues raised through the performance the previous steps utilizing the Pareto principle where the most significant areas for improvement are addressed first followed by succeeding levels of criticality. The guiding principle of this process is to completely correct problems to minimize reoccurrence. Leaders instill intense staff commitment to identify root causes and institute clear steps to rectify the problem.

Step Seven: A strategy is developed to identify critical success factors to strive towards Zero Defects for all organization products and/or services. This becomes the basis of a program built around clear action steps designed to build "ZD" commitment across the organization. Key components include explaining the program to all levels of management, identifying preparation materials and launch methods, highlighting critical action steps, establishing recognition methods, complete scheduling, and finalizing execution plans. The "battle cry" throughout the organization "do it right the first time" where everyone is focusing attention on tasks to minimize incorrect actions versus just get it done because someone else will clean up errors.

The remaining steps focus on implementation of the quality improvement process with full integration into the daily operations of an organization. Organization leaders are fully trained on key elements of the program and briefed prior to launch. The entire organization is then oriented on the zero defect goal and the critical steps to be implemented which will result in significant positive change. Shortly after this event specific goals and objectives are established through all levels of the organization. To aid this performance management effort a problem solving system is established to overcome major roadblocks to progress. Individual and group accomplishments are regularly recognized when specific goals and milestones are achieved and individuals at all levels understand that management seriously needs their assistance plus sincerely appreciates the results. Leadership constantly reinforces that the TQM program is never ending with each milestone setting the stage for new goals to be achieved.

Crosby stressed that it took five to seven years of unrelenting effort to achieve a major change in the organization culture at ITT. With planning, hard work, and unwavering top management commitment/involvement the company became a recognized quality management leader. It is clearly an example of how significant organization effectiveness improvement can be accomplished utilizing specific measurement benchmarks for success.

Organization Reengineering

One of the most recent organization design and change methodologies was put forth by Michael Hammer and James Champy which has become known as organization reengineering. In their book *Reengineering the Corporation* (1993) they stress that most American companies are about to enter the twenty-first century using a nineteenth century organization model and demonstrate how leaders can radically redesign processes, structure, and culture. The authors provide a vision on how organizations can make a quantum leap in performance rather than the incremental improvements associated with TQM to be successful or even survive in the 90's and beyond.

The most critical aspect of the reengineering process is to move away from historic principles on how to organize work which date back to the Industrial Revolution. The authors contend that the long standing bureaucratic structure and antiquated control systems can no longer meet the requirements of global competition and fast paced change. As a replacement, they offer the demonstrated success of the use of process orientation that examines and modifies start to finish activities that create value for customers. Organization results are highlighted which provide a guide for creating a new form of organization in a new industrial environment.

They observed based on their involvement with a wide variety of corporations that most industrial organizations continue to utilize the structure which evolved in the 1950s and 1960s. Similar to the theme discussed earlier in this book, most organizations took a comfortable form based on the collective past experience of key members without much analysis or interest in changing well tested principles. Customers, Competition, and Change were all driving organization leaders away from past methods toward flexibility and quick response. Rather than an over reliance on finding the right products and services the emphasis must shift to development of required processes that create products for long term success. The key to this success is a clear understanding of how day-to-day work gets done and learning how to do it better.

The essence of the Hammer & Champy message is that organizing with a focus on tasks is obsolete and must be replaced by a focus on the work process. Leaders who understand the difference can leap ahead of their competition by reinventing the organization. Most companies consist of narrowly focused functional fiefdoms with minimal concern for the customer. The authors recognized the root cause of America's business problem as the use of a nineteenth century organization design to meet twentieth century requirements and stressed that something very different will be needed in the twenty-first century.

They go on to clearly describe the fundamentals of reengineering which starts with the requirement that everyone involved need to carefully examine the underlying principles that drive the way they conduct their businesses by focusing on what should be rather than the current accepted methodology. The next critical element is radical redesign with total disregard for existing structures and procedures where methods for accomplishing required work are invented. In addition, dramatic improvement is implemented where quantum leaps in performance are accomplished rather than incremental adjustment. Most important is the emphasis on process development which includes the analysis of all activities that require various types of input and create some output valued by a customer. Primarily, reengineering is geared toward reversing the industrial revolution where division of labor, hierarchical control, and economies of scale were paramount and searching for new models for the organization of work.

Hammer & Champy highlight a number of success stories where companies such as Hallmark, Taco Bell, and Bell Atlantic reengineered their organization and in all cases senior managers clearly communicated to the workforce where they were as an enterprise and the vision for the future. This became a launch point and the effort became a top priority throughout the company. Success was achieved 30–50% of the time when the leadership remained focused on several critical success factors. These included change to critical processes rather than trying for a quick fix, a clear awareness of the big picture, attention to people's values and beliefs, a constant push for major results, change remaining a long term effort, broad scope for the program, leadership commitment to change, full understanding of reengineering at all levels, invest in sufficient resources, keep reengineering at the top of the corporate agenda, continue to prioritize projects, continue to differentiate the effort from other improvement programs, concentrate on both design and implementation, persistently overcome resistance, and set clear parameters for completion of no more than a year to move problem identification to new process implementation.

For those that fail, the primary cause could usually be traced to a lack of understanding or leadership at the senior executive level but spectacular results were realized when they sounded the call for action.

This brings us very near to the end of the twentieth century and as we can see there is a tremendous wealth of ideas, scientific evidence, theories, success stories and dramatic failures relating to the history of the organization. Hopefully, our tracing of this evolution from the earliest social units surviving during prehistoric times to contemporary global corporations has created a fuller appreciation of organizational behavior fundamentals. So let's move on to a review of several practical examples of methods that have led to organization success.

6

EFFECTIVE ORGANIZATION

○ ○
"Prove all things; hold fast that which is good."

—I Thessalonians

Throughout history the organization has been utilized as a tool to aid the survival of social groups, win epoch battles between opposing forces, ensure the growth and continuity of religious teachings, and expand vast economic enterprises. It has been demonstrated that organization structure and dynamics occur naturally throughout a variety animal species, have been successfully and unsuccessfully applied by most groups of humans as society has evolved, and remains very mystifying or misunderstood as we move into the 21st century. Several recent literary works that fall outside the more traditional study of organizational principles provide further valuable insight into the influence of organization success factors.

It is my intent to review this very current historical snap shot and develop a unified organizational theory which can be linked to the pragmatic application of organizational analysis techniques. In the early 60's, a leading organization theorist Amitai Etzioni, developed an exhaustive review of studies conducted by experts in the field of organization analysis which provides an exceptional model for the formulation of a usable theory. (Etzioni, 1961) He stressed that the critical focus of organization theory was finding the balance between rational and non-rational demonstrations of human behavior found in society and human thought. Understanding optimum methods for the coordination of human activities which result in a highly rational unit, social integration, plus reasonable commitment and motivation of organization participants forms a foundation for such a theory. He highlighted the theory developed by Talcott Parsons who was one of the leading researchers to develop modern methods of organizational analysis. This model defines an organization as a system which produces specific results based on defined goals where members of the social unit comprehend that a common purpose and shared values exist. This orientation guides the activities of participants to prioritize organization results over individual interests and legitimize defined roles within the unit such as line authority or support staff. Utilizing this model, we can explore contemporary historical and scientific research and formulate a usable organization theory to further guide the development of organization effectiveness.

Biological Model

A renowned scientist, Rupert Sheldrake, developed a new and radically expansive concept of how and why nature evolved using a combined historical, philosophical, and scientific thought process. He further explored how this evolution impacted biology, psychology, society, and culture and how these concepts can increase the understanding of human behavior and our environment. (Sheldrake,1995) Rather than focusing on the "why" which is based in his theory that memory inherently exists in nature, we will concentrate how this evolution has impacted the very natural occurrence of recognizable organization throughout nature.

It is striking how he describes the fact that all animal species demonstrate a very natural predisposition for patterns of organization and coordination. These social structures range from very simple where males and females come together during the reproductive period to highly complex social units formed by termites and chimpanzees. Studies of more complex organizations have documented well defined role hierarchies and the highly coordinated activities demonstrated in the hunting techniques of a wolf pack. Most researchers agree that a high level of social order exists and occurs very naturally within most animal species. Sheldrake successfully demonstrates that individual behavior is well coordinated within defined social units throughout nature and further applies these principles to human societies and cultures.

Primates

One of the best examples of a naturally occurring social structure is those observed through the study of the behavior of our closest animal relative the chimpanzee. Jane Goodall has devoted over 30 years of research to effectively document similarities between chimpanzee and human behavior which includes communication patterns, tool-using/making, cooperative hunting, and organized warfare. (Goodall, 1990) The most complex social configuration that parallels the study of human organizations is their practice of warfare which she defines as organized armed conflict between groups. Her descriptions of well coordinated, aggressive behavior similar to primitive human warfare where chimpanzees stalk the enemy and demonstrate cooperative hunting skills with use of weapons reinforces this natural occurrence of organizational characteristics. She observed that the chimpanzees would congregate in distinct communities with defined territories and when encounters occur open conflict takes place. There appears to be clearly defined roles within attacking bands with well coordinated tactics designed to isolate opponents and severely attack each helpless victim. A high degree of emotion and an ability to seize opportunities were constantly demonstrated to achieve their goal. When a community would achieve victory, the defeated group would successfully launch a well coordinated retreat into further removed and smaller territory.

An even more recent account the natural organization ability of chimpanzees is included in psychologist and primate researcher Roger

Fouts book *Next of Kin* (1997). He further documents, with scientifically sound examples, how our closest animal relatives that share 98.4% of the same DNA as humans demonstrate communication, tool-making, abstract thought and other characteristics required for organized behavior. His work has been viewed as one of the most profound research efforts since those completed by Darwin. The research was based on Fout's success teaching chimpanzees American Sign Language which provided them with a means of communicating with humans and among themselves. The depth of emotion, understanding, and cognitive ability demonstrated further establishes the species as an ideal subject for the study of the natural occurrence of organized behavior.

The book traces over thirty years of this very personalized experience working with individuals and groups of chimpanzees which graphically illustrates the many similarities between them and us. There are also numerous accounts of extremely joyful experiences and tremendous heartbreak. In addition to describing the individuality and intelligence of chimpanzees, Fouts observed and reported a well defined chimpanzee culture. He also uncovered numerous research discoveries that demonstrate that chimpanzee communities have their own unique hunter-gatherer cultures where tools identical to those used by humans were utilized.

In 1996, he traveled to Africa to witness this culture firsthand which he viewed as one of the peak experiences of his life. For several hours they tracked the group up rocky hills, through dense brush, and down deep ravines. He was amazed by how swiftly and well organized the community navigated through the jungle and their ability to process information in simultaneous fashion. They maintained constant awareness of the location of family, social group, potential enemies, and their planned destination. It became very obvious that the chimpanzee social unit was far superior to their human cousins when traveling and achieving required goals in this very challenging environment. All the activities observed such as hunting, food gathering, training of children, recreation, and use of tools were very natural and well organized. His accounts of this extremely profound experience further reinforces the natural occurrence of organized behavior within the social units of these close human relatives which directly translated to a similar capability within the human species.

Organized Religion

As civilization evolved, early formalized organizations were taking shape as the world's leading religions were being formed. In the book *A History of God*, Karen Armstrong traces the changes in religion from earliest human history, medieval mysticism, Reformation, and Enlightenment to the modern age. (Armstrong, 1993) It appears that belief in a deity or deities grows out of the effort by human beings to explain the mystery and tragedy of life and creating them is something humans have always done. The early symbolic stories, cave paintings and carvings were an attempt to explain natural phenomena and personalize the mystery they perceived. These ideas began to emerge roughly 14,000 years ago when people attempted to express a sense of purpose and affinity with the uncontrollable world around them where the supernatural realm represented an ideal to which people could aspire. God or Gods were credited with the direction to humans which provided the design for their cities and temples which were replicas of structure in the divine world. In 4000 BC the Sumerians established one of the earliest organized civilizations which included writing, ornate temples, progressive laws, literature, and mythology. During the period 800–200 BC termed the Axial age, many of these concepts crystallized into new ideologies which were the foundation of new religious systems across all regions of the civilized world. This led to profound social changes where power shifted from kings/priests to the merchant class. These new ideologies created a reason to elevate humans as highly valued beings and provided a sense of purpose for much of organized society.

All of the world's prominent religions began with a small group that had a profound sense of purpose and belief in common values which elevated human existence, placing increased importance on the development mankind as full human beings. In 722 BC, the small Kingdom of Judah led by the prophet Isaiah, who held populist and democratic views, began to establish an ideology where the belief in one God became the central source of meaning and protection to their civilization. Seven hundred years later, Jesus, who became the corner stone of the Christian religion, quoted Isaiah and many Jews believed that he was the Messiah who would be the founder of a new Israel. He and his small group of disciples developed a huge following of believers and after his death they concluded that Jesus was divine. His teachings became the ideology which was carried to Jews and non-Jews throughout the middle-east by St. Paul and other disciples and became the foundation of the massive institution that exists today. During the period when the Jewish religion was being formalized, Muhammad experienced a divine revelation while observing Ramadan. He was roused from sleep by a deep sense of divine presence and he began to recite the first scriptures which became the basis of the Koran. In this sacred book, God explains the significance of conflicts within the early Muslim community and highlights the divine nature of human life. When he died in 632 BC, he successfully brought most tribes of Arabia into a new united community that held the common belief that Muslims had a duty to create a just society where everyone was treated decently.

From these simple yet profound beginnings, each of these religions survived, grew, and became a central driving force throughout most civilizations. Each provided purpose, values, and historical identity in the cultures where they thrived. By the end of the sixteenth century the Renaissance had occurred in Europe, the New World had been discovered, a scientific revolution was underway, and significant cultural changes were taking place. During this period Islam had become a dominant force in the world and several new empires were founded.

The Christian religion had split into Catholic and Protestant factions which generated tremendous conflict throughout Europe. The Jewish religion had migrated to many locations and maintained a distinctive culture in the midst of both Catholic or Muslim dominated societies. What is even more impressive concerning the influence of religious values on human existence was the fact that no society in the world had successfully eliminated religion. The organization principles demonstrated the phenomenal growth and survival of these religious sects were purpose, clear shared values, written documentation of history and belief structure, and numerous leaders that carried the banner at critical periods of growth and evaluation.

It has also been demonstrated that these characteristics which led to the growth and influence of religion during the evolution of civilization could have been instrumental in the actual preservation of the great heritage developed by early civilization. The fall of the Roman Empire led to the disappearance of most learning, philosophy, literature, and culture included in recorded Greek, Roman, Jewish, and Christian works. In the book *How the Irish Saved Civilization* (Cahill, 1995) the events leading up to the fall of Rome and the efforts which saved these cultural treasures are well documented and artfully described.

It is ironic that one of the most dominating and longest lasting civilizations that developed exceptional capabilities in husbandry, agriculture, horticulture, cuisine, arts, literature, philosophy, law, politics, and military science could fall. Most of the historians cited stressed that the decline was very gradual and remained unnoticed by members of the society. The culmination of the decline occurred when a huge mass of barbarian German tribes invaded across the frozen Rhine and burned, looted, raped, and murdered to successfully destroy Roman civilization. It's amazing that the polished and highly disciplined Roman soldiers could not hold back this crudely dressed, dirty, foul smelling horde that lacked organization or any regard for personal survival.

A number of organizational elements eroded during this period of decline which greatly increased the possibilities for social destruction. The social purpose and commitment to early social values were lost and the quality standards for army recruits were greatly reduced. Most formal organizations became increasingly unwieldy and highly bureaucratic while wealth became more and more concentrated within a very small segment of the populace.

As the classical culture died, a much more basic barbarian way of life took control where people didn't read, think about lofty concepts or build beautiful structures. The population struggled to survive during this chaotic era and clung to a desire for the rule of law. The one social structure that survived during this upheaval was the Roman Catholic bishop leadership position. After the death of the apostles, most early Christian congregations were led by priests or bishops appointed by each local congregation.

During this period, small monastic communities were established in various regions of Ireland that began to attract people from a vast area of Europe. Each was surrounded by a simple wall which enclosed small drystone huts shaped like a beehive with a tiny church in the middle of the community. People would journey great distances to sit at the feet of the monks, learn Greek and Latin literature, religious teachings and listen to ancient stories. The lifestyle was extremely simple and all who came were welcomed with books, teaching, and food. This rich learning environment assumed a very unique role in the history of Western culture where the monks began to transcribe Greek, Roman, and Biblical literature. These ornate Irish manuscripts which captured most of the classical writings from this medieval period are today icons in libraries throughout East/West Europe.

One of the keys to the viability of this society was the simple community structure and guidelines for expansion. Whenever the monastery reached the level of 150 monks, a group of 13 would set out to establish another community in a new setting utilizing the same simple layout of earlier groups. By the end of the sixth century 60 communities had been established where monks continued to teach, study, pray, farm, and transcribe most classical literary works. This model for expansion continued across Europe and many of the monasteries evolved into great European cities. The resiliency of religious organizations continues to be demonstrated as we look back to their evolution and observe them as they exist today. The dynamics of these modern institutions provide excellent insight into many organizational characteristics studied throughout our historical exploration.

Large Scale Warfare

Military challenges have also created a need for organized activity throughout the historical evolution of human society. Organized warfare has existed from the earliest recorded accounts during the prehistoric period to the modern technology driven conflict we have all witnessed. In her book *Blood Rites*, Barbara Ehrenreich traces this evolution from the dawn of human civilization on the plains of Africa to today's highly mechanized and globally mobile military organization. (Ehrenreich, 1997)

Through her review of the study of early human society, it is clear that hominids evolved as social beings as a defense against predators where groups were bound together to ensure collective protection. The research indicates that military technology and organization grew out of techniques developed by prehistoric humans to hunt animals. An excellent example of this is the line advance used by light regiments well into modern times which is very similar to methods used by Paleolithic hunters in their drives against animals. History has shown that these hunting methods also include highly ritualized activity connected to social group recognition and leadership authority. The earliest recorded human warfare centered around raids to steal animal herds and grew into systematic conflict where animal herders discovered that a raid on agricultural communities was more efficient than development of their own food supply. The earliest recorded warrior was the Sumerian Gilgamesh known also as a hunter and battler of predatory animals and Greek heroes were all known as hunters of wild animals. From this beginning, military conflict spread throughout most human cultures and required that societies become prepared for war with weapons, organization, and manpower to match those of any potential enemy or attacker.

As military structure became a critical component of most primitive societies, it imposed a variety of organizational requirements. Weapons must be developed, logistical methods need to be established to obtain materials, a complex division of labor is required with centralized command systems, and more formalized political structures become the norm. This need for military capability greatly influenced the forms of social organization that evolved and placed significant demands on human cultures.

During the 15th to 18th century, military methods and organization changed to include more sophisticated weapons and large formalized armies. Weapons began to be mass produced which led to greatly increased fighting unit size and impersonal combat. Countries formed large standing armies even during peaceful periods that were ready to defend against or attack enemies which necessitated rigid methods of organization and control. This resulted in the development of the bureaucratized officer role responsible for the direction and training of the troops. Drills included rank formation, use of weapons, and battle tactics and many operations were segmented into simplified steps to maximize organization efficiency very similar to the methodology promoted by Frederich Taylor years later.

Ehrenreich contends that these changes to military structure led to the emergence of the modern bureaucratic state. The need to support a large army stimulated the development of commerce requiring central state authority to enforce contracts and manage well defined systems for currency and measurement. What resulted were numerous nation-states with central land management and productive support systems. Throughout history the military organization has been constantly redefined yet the basic structure has remained organized along the same hierarchical lines as mass armies from the past.

We can now reflect on the common theme that emerges through the historical exploration of fundamental organization components that impact the effectiveness of social units within the context of current applications being practiced throughout contemporary organizations. Numerous examples exist that illuminate successful methods utilized to better organize and channel the efforts within social units to maximize results.

In the next chapter we will look at several different companies through the eyes of the chief executive and determine how they launch and build effective organization efforts.

7

CEO EXPERIENCE

Each company tends to apply organization principles in their own unique fashion to aid and support the accomplishment of strategic goals. It is critical that organization leaders have a basic understanding of each key element being utilized to impact overall organization effectiveness. Usually organization structure and methodology evolves as a result of environmental impact, leadership priorities, and staff interactions.

One of the optimum ways to better understand these principles that have been refined over the years, is to share in the experiences of organization leaders who have applied many of the techniques highlighted throughout this book. To gain this insight meetings were held during 2000 with several company presidents and key points summarized. Each case study reports the position and company information at that point in time.

Pfizer

We begin with the experiences discussed with George Milne, PhD. the President of Pfizer Central Research. One of the greatest challenges he faces is to continue building on the tremendous basic research success achieved over the previous 20 years. It is well recognized that this organization is the life blood of the company.

Pfizer, a $13.5 billion dollar pharmaceutical company, has been powered to one of *Fortune's* most admired companies by the quality of its leadership and the quality of its drug discovery pipeline. George Milne, the president of Central Research for the previous five years, stands high on the list of Pfizer executives responsible for its superstar performance.

During the five years, Central Research's productivity more than doubled. Pfizer is solidly in the first tier of all pharmaceutical companies and one of the most fearsome competitors, for top pharmaceutical talent, able to attract the best and the brightest. Its own employees reportedly comment about the stimulation and motivation of working at Pfizer Central Research. Few can imagine working anywhere else.

Pfizer Central Research is no small organization. It spreads across three major sites: Groton, CT; Sandwich, UK; and Nagoya, Japan, and employs 7,000 people. Pfizer's R&D budget is one of the industries largest at 2.8B for 1999. Meanwhile, a broad growth program is underway that is designed to further expand this engine of Pfizer success.

To accomplish this, Dr. Milne is committed to a clearly articulated organizational philosophy that includes the following five principles that are relevant to the themes of this book:

- Creating alignment around aggressive visionary goals

- Building shared values

- Managing by spotlight

- Recognizing and rewarding contributions

- Enhancing scholarship

Creating Alignment

Pfizer and Central Research have their eyes on sustained leadership and what Dr. Milne calls a constant "ambition for excellence". This means setting high, visionary goals across all the dimensions required to sustain leadership—productivity, attracting and retaining the very best people, outlearning the competition, living the values, technical leadership and goal-setting that lives in the organization.

After division-wide goals are set, George Milne leads a process that cascades each goal throughout all levels. His direct reports take the goals and define their groups' contribution. This process continues through all levels so that everyone sees their connection to business success.

The process isn't one way. Each level is expected to question, enrich and sharpen the goals it receives. As a result, the final set of goals reflects the entire alignment process. Achieving alignment builds trust and facilitates communication as each group also shares their goals with the groups with whom they interact.

Building Shared Values

A sense of shared values is fundamental to organizational cohesion. As such, Dr. Milne has initiated the steps necessary to build and reinforce shared values, which reflect his own values and those of all employees. These values include continuous improvement of Performance, Teamwork, Leadership, Innovation, Respect for People, Integrity, Customer Focus, and improvement to Country and Community.

These values were affirmed after an eight month employee survey process which included feedback discussion at all levels of the organization. Once finalized, the values were communicated throughout the organization using a comprehensive process that began with a meeting where all George's direct reports were briefed on the importance of the resulting values.

A year later Pfizer conducted a Values Survey to determine how well the organization "lived" its values. Though employee satisfaction was an amazing 78%, the Central Research Division is committed to addressing areas where feedback was less positive. In addition, the feedback went to each supervisor who respond within their organization unit.

Also, the top 150 people within the research hierarchy spent two days describing, discussing and committing to behaviors that demonstrate that they consistently "walk the talk". Individual participants were provided confidential feedback on how well they were doing and Dr. Milne requested and received ongoing feedback on his performance in living the values.

Managing by Spotlight

George knows that his areas of focus will elicit the attention of others. He believes that the "Hawthorne Effect" is perhaps the single most powerful and reliable area of management awareness. Simple as it sounds, if he stops to pick up litter in the hallway so will others and this sends a message throughout the organization concerning respect for quality and community values. If he makes a point of asking about new ideas, generating new ideas will get more attention. If he shows concern for an employee's time away from home, others will look at the balance of time at work. He uses his "spotlight" judiciously to reinforce the values, goals, and major initiatives of the organization. For example, if a group is meeting to discuss developing "stretch" goals, something he strongly endorses, he will, if invited, attend the meeting to offer support and encouragement.

He also uses questions effectively. In presentations about the progress of promising new drugs in the research pipelines, he will always ask about health and safety side-affects. In anticipation of his insightful questions, his staff will be even more critical in evaluating and preparing their information.

Recognizing and Rewarding All Contributions

Dr. Milne hand-writes 30–40 notes a week which range from thanking people who set up chairs for a meeting to recognizing significant scientific achievements and these notes are seen posted in hundreds of offices. What the notes communicate is his philosophy that everyone contributes to the success of the enterprise without regard to job or level in the organization where no task is too small and no job unimportant.

He personally interacts with employees by constantly walking into labs and chatting. Whenever possible, he will grab lunch in the cafeteria and simply sit at a table of employees he does not know and begin talking with them.

Enhancing Scholarship

Everyone is expected to test assumptions, ask questions and look for patterns with a sense of restless curiosity. In plans and budgets he expects to see resources directed to "scholarship," i.e., learning more about areas of importance to Pfizer's business and provides financial support in the form of travel budgets for conferences and seminars, external research contracts and outside experts. People are not expected to have "all the answers"; they are expected to ask the key questions and to look for the answers.

As a part of scholarship, George expects everyone to have a career development plan that focuses on their professional growth. He again supports this with ample resources for internal and external educational activities.

These five fundamental principles are used to challenge, improve and maximize the success of the organization and build on its success. Each pillar forms the foundation for his leadership role and shapes his leadership agenda.

Concord Communications

One of the best examples of pragmatic application of basic organization principles were those implemented by Jack Blaeser, President of Concord Communications. Since early 1996 he has successfully transformed this company, which was struggling at the time, into a market leader in the development of IS system monitoring software. Earlier in his career he was President of a company that invented the programmable controller (Modicon) which led to a Corporate Vice President role following the purchase of the company by Gould Electronics. He began his career at GE and was a peer of Jack Welch. He recently finished reading Welch's latest book and has incorporated several of the ideas to reinforce many of the key initiatives that have been critical to the success of the organization. Jack reads continuously and usually has a contemporary business book with him while travelling or in the office.

Over the past three years he has kept his team focused on several organization goals which he believes have been critical to the success they have experienced. A very high priority is placed on constant vigilance to ensure that the caliber of individuals brought into the company are top quality. As the organization has grown Jack has remained involved in the hiring process and demonstrates leadership by working very hard to directly impact hiring success. He takes every possible opportunity to reinforce results and remind those making decisions of the critical nature of this goal.

In addition, equal emphasis is placed on listening very carefully to customer input and development of a high integrity relationship with each of them. This includes a high level of employee and customer involvement in product development and upgrades. Staff at all organization levels review development plans and maintain a continuous dialog with customers. Monthly user group meetings are held to constantly update their needs or wants and product beta tests are managed by product development staff.

Most user group meetings are led by Jack and the Vice President of Engineering. The primary goal is to build rapport with those attending to reinforce trust and insure that all critical needs are communicated. One of the greatest builders of trust is demonstrating a consistently high level of reliability where realistic targets are established with actual delivery results that are consistent with commitments. Their success speaks for itself with a 10% increase in their customer base quarterly. Their very open, participative, operating style is reinforces both internally and externally. It is quite common to have engineers argue very vigorously for improved product functionality and they are constantly pushing the customer needs envelope.

These methods and techniques are a dramatic change from those practiced prior to Jack assuming the role of President. There was limited involvement of staff in organization decisions and overall coordination of organization efforts and company focus needed to be greatly improved. His initial emphasis was to clearly define the company's business charter and evaluate market potential. The Board of Directors then approved the company revitalization plan.

Staff Involvement

Several programs have been established to support the combined business plan, customer focus, and staff quality initiatives. Since going public in October 1997 all staff members have become shareholders. Each year that the company meets or exceeds its business goals all employees with partners included are treated to a group vacation trip which receives extensive media attention most years in New England. A very interactive team culture is reinforced where loyalty, excitement, enjoyment of the work efforts are all paramount and career and financial rewards are significant. Each year the entire staff is evaluated and those not keeping pace receive coaching to improve performance or they are moved out of the organization. Most staff have office space and the work environment is modern and upbeat. There is a vital sense of mutual ownership based on a clear sense of business purpose plus an understanding throughout the organization of key business targets. Everyone is on a mission to support delivery and fix customer concerns.

Planning Builds Teams

One of the most valuable management tools which facilitates their dramatic 100% per year growth rate is a bottom/up team budget process. Cross functional joint goals are established each business cycle and all managers are empowered to distribute necessary resources. Tremendous emphasis is placed to the development and enhancement of excellent team chemistry and effectiveness. This is clearly understood by leaders to be a top organization priority.

Jack projects several key future organization initiatives to continue the tremendous growth and success experienced by Concord Communication over the last three years.

A paramount organization priority will be placed on the continuous reinforcement of a well understood mission by the entire staff. With their rapid growth rate, it will become increasingly more difficult to monitor this level of understanding and support to leverage the momentum that currently exists. It is Jack's goal to develop a mechanism which will provide an accurate calibration of this support.

Their efforts must be strengthened by the consistent development of a common language to facilitate this understanding and the flow of communications. The sense of a common pursuit, mutual trust, and focus on a few well defined goals are consistently redefined through effective utilization of this common language.

To further build momentum, more formal training will be implemented in addition to the informal methods that have been highly successful up to this point. The willingness of managers and experienced staff to coach and train those needing development has been a valuable asset, however, with increased growth a more formal approach will be required.

At the core of their developmental efforts, remains the very open, highly participative, and strong customer orientation organization culture that has fueled growth during the past three years. Similar to Pfizer, leaders value an ideal of stewardship to ensure that this environment is nurtured and passed on to all new and existing staff. Jack is convinced that these values will insure continued growth and business success.

Schneider

The next example highlights an extremely challenging organization environment where the application of well matched organization principles are critical. For the past three years, Ray Sansouci has been President of Schneider Automation, Inc. which has combined the industrial automation businesses of four companies (Merlin Gerin, Modicon, Square D, Telemecanique). Not only is this a meshing of four corporate cultures but also U.S. and European cultures. Ray has spent most of his career in the automation industry since being recruited from the Harvard Business School campus by Gould Electronics to be a Product Manager for their Industrial Automation Group in the early 80's. Prior to joining Group Schneider he held senior marketing/sales executive positions with Texas Instruments, Siemens, and the Automation Group of Damler Benz.

Ray views the dramatic shift by industry to a commerce as the most significant factor affecting organization structure and staff interaction. He cites Dell Computer and Amazon.com as paramount examples of this transformation.

One book that stands out of the many he has read, is *Cyber Corp* by James Martin which highlights this systems revolution and its impact on organizations. The infrastructure relied upon over the last 20 years to meet the needs of global enterprise is rapidly losing effectiveness.

Information Processing

Information brokers stand to lose much of their influence as a result of the very free flow of information brought about by electronic systems. They tend to see the shift as a threat and often resist or retard the change process. Those interested in maintaining power and control will tend to protect the status quo, however Ray believes that the shift is underway and the major transformation is inevitable.

Strategically, Schneider Automation, has developed as a corner stone for the development of their business, a state-of-the-art Marketing Information System. Enterprise, as it is called, links customers and organization staff in an electronic virtual organization. This is a first critical step in the revision of the organization infrastructure. Parallel to this development, market data is rapidly being gathered to better understand the impact of the internet on the industrial automation industry. He recently learned from a variety of sources at Harvard Business School that none of the best thinkers that focus on the topic have a clear projection on what will occur.

The underlying foundation of several organization initiatives is the application of McGregor's Theory X or Y assumptions concerning basic worker values. Throughout his career, Ray has held views compatible with Theory Y where people truly are motivated to perform in a way that is consistent with organization goals as they understand them. He strongly believes that a Theory X assumption is inaccurate and views such an attitude as a negative influence on the results of any organization.

The fundamental principle guiding the efforts of Schneider Automation, is the clear communication and reinforcement of goal results planned and expected. With defined expectations most people will work very hard to get the results needed for personal and organization success. To support these efforts, staff at all levels understand that they have full immunity from management rules that do not support established goals.

Commitment to change has been reinforced through organization support of the new automated information systems. The availability of information on-line is clearly communicated to internal and external customers. When then they seek hard copy, they are guided to the electronic system and if the request persists it is refused.

Heavy emphasis is placed on removal of the blinders many people establish to shield awareness of critical organization priorities. The most difficult challenge is keeping the staff focused on the correct measures for business success. In the past, too much emphasis was placed on production or product measures rather than a clear understanding of critical customer requirements. They now have a goal to implement product ideas developed based on thorough analysis of expressed customer needs which remain as close to the original concept as possible.

To accomplish this goal a team has been established that melds customer hotline staff, technical development, and customer support. The entire team understands and identifies with the purpose of their role, which is the "champion" of customer expectations. The organization is very flat, meets regularly via video conferencing technology, and customer support staff positions have been elevated to be higher level in the organization. Engineers communicate directly with customers and customer metrics rather than production drive the entire business. All other segments of the organization are built around this core entity.

Ray likes to use an athletic analogy when describing the essence of his role as President. He leads the development of a clear achievable plan, coaches organizations members to optimize professional growth and business results, and insures that understandable score keeping is accomplished and communicated. He has found that creative vision emanating from he and his staff develops a sense of purpose throughout Schneider Automation with strong commitment at all levels.

Effective use of these organization techniques should aid the connection of the diverse cultures and successfully build the business. The combined customer focus and e-commerce orientation should position Schneider Automation as a significant player in their industry.

Citibank

Shifting our focus away from the technology oriented arena to the very dynamic financial services industry; an extremely informative meeting was held with Mr. Carlos Palomares, Chairman of Citibank International, Latin America Consumer Bank. Prior to assuming this leadership role two years ago, he was President of Citibank, Florida for several years.

Similar to the other Chief Executives previously discussed, Carlos is also an avid reader in the areas of science, classical history, and business. When he has the time for pure reading for pleasure, most of the books selected will cover various periods of history. His early mathematical training has led to a continuous application of the physical sciences to enhance business success. Most significantly, he has utilized this discipline to remain open minded and follow a scientific thought process to arrive at solutions to address business challenges and organization effectiveness.

He, George Milne, and Bruce Rusch, President of Analogic who will be highlighted later in this chapter, all stated that Peter Drucker stands out over most other organization management leaders that have become well known over the last 20 years. The primary reason for this recognition is his insight concerning the theory of management, extensive exploration and description of the managerial role in an organization and continuous study and definition of fundamental management skills. In addition, Carlos referenced Michael Portor and most importantly his book *Competitive Analysis* as another valuable resource.

In line with the corporate leaders already highlighted he has also applied several very fundamental management principles to build organization success.

Vision

The principle that Carlos views as being extremely valuable to organizational success is an initiative focused on development of a clear and well understood "vision" which stresses targets of opportunity and pragmatic critical success factors. A common mistake that must be avoided are grandiose projections which lack meaningful connection to viable results which concentrate on form versus substance. The vision needs to be articulated in a manner that is understood throughout the organization to become a rallying point for the front line and all other levels.

Even though the bank is part of the service industry, he has found the use of a manufacturing industry model an excellent tool to aid the implementation of the visioning process. He recalled how Kamatsu, the large Japanese Construction Equipment company, took well-defined steps to capture market share from Caterpillar. Each day every-one in the company established a very specific objective and would assemble every morning to proclaim "Kill Caterpillar". Another example would be for a company losing money where the rallying call might be "We must break even next year". For Jack Blaeser at Concord Communications, the message for a year was "Go Public next October". Included in this very active communication effort is continuous feed back to all on the progress toward the desired results. It is critical that the fundamental mission direction is understood throughout the organization with actual progress points described as the effort unfolds.

The vision needs to be reinforced by the identification and communication of values placed in high esteem by the leadership of a social unit. The entire staff tends to be aware either formally or informally how these values are exhibited. Consistency between observed behavior and stated expectations is critical when establishing a model for leadership. This is particularly vital for the Chief Executive because it sets the standard for the entire leadership group.

Customer Focus

For Citibank, the core focus for the enterprise is the continuous building of each customer's trust in the bank's ability to aid their financial well being. This requires diligence to insure that a balance is maintained between satisfying customer needs and business profitability goals. With a combined organization effort toward understanding and meeting customer needs the result is the growth of customer loyalty.

The management tool that Carlos has continued to find most useful is a well-tuned objective setting process. Most critical to the overall success of goal setting is an emphasis on the "critical few" results which will have the greatest impact on success for the business. They need to be clear on well aligned across the organization. He has found the Balanced Scorecard methodology, developed at Harvard Business School, very helpful to establish common measures to calibrate results and facilitate the alignment effort. It is important to include supporting activities such as people management and community involvement as key components of the measurable results sought. Too heavy a focus on strict bottom line success can detract from the broader efforts required.

Carlos foresees that future organization development initiatives will be the strengthening of staff capabilities to work in conjunction with all organization units. Careful attention will be placed on reduction of the "Silo" effect, which naturally creeps into most organizations where each functional area is internally focused with little awareness of the efforts of other functions. This need has been further amplified by the merger with Travelers to form Citigroup and the explosive globalization of the industry. It has become increasingly critical that everyone leverage or aid other parts of the organization to achieve necessary results.

The hierarchical structure with narrowly defined responsibilities relied upon in the past no longer functions effectively in the current rapidly changing global business environment. Organization leaders who rely on a command and control style of management have become much less successful than those who have gained the capability of "working through people". Carlos has led an initiative to develop the management skills necessary to orchestrate the required shift in leadership methods.

Carlos also views the effective utilization of emerging technology as a tool to facilitate the way that organization staff functions rather than an additional activity to burden the organization. As Citigroup develops plans for success in the 21st Century, the key challenge is to develop new models to insure effectiveness. Most of the critical success factors identified over the last 5–10 years no longer appear to apply. Enterprises that emulate small entrepreneurial ventures have demonstrated phenomenal impact on the global economy.

We as corporate leaders must totally rethink business structure and methods and no clear answers are evident. Each planning cycle the company examines their five major competitors and the profile has totally changed over the last five years. Companies that establish the strongest link to customer will be industry leaders. Now companies such as Microsoft, Internet, and AOL are in the top five rather than traditional financial institutions. They must combat the risk of becoming a service commodity! One clear trend that stands out in the rapid evolution occurring is the constant building of strategic alliances. Many other structures and methods must also be formulated to strengthen organizational effectiveness.

Analogic

Bruce Rusch, President of Analogic, provides us with a very interesting view of a key player in the Hardware/Software Systems Integration industry. The company develops a wide range of technologies, which are applied to a variety of Fortune 50 Corporate products. (e.g. GE, Siemens). They ask the customer to describe what they need and Analogic will develop a creative engineering and/or manufacturing solution. A recent example of their success was development of a portable CAT Scanner that fit very tight price and profit parameters.

Bruce joined Analogic several years ago through the acquisition of Sky Computer, a company he built as CEO, which developed and marketed high-end super computers. The two companies have meshed well and the added high speed computing capability has further enhanced company success.

He has practiced several organization principles from his vantage point as Chief Executive to enhance organization effectiveness.

In concert with several of the other executives discussed, he formulates and communicates his Vision that highlights strategic direction and future possibilities for the organization. The areas stressed are grounded in reality while providing uplifting direction to focus staff efforts. Imbedded in the vision is a Mission Statement that describes organization values, guidelines for action, and description of core business focus. (e.g. develop creative engineering/manufacturing solutions to meet critical corporate customer needs). This Vision should resonate throughout the organization while creating a sense of belief at all levels. This frame of reference is particularly critical as the pace of change continues to increase by establishing a rallying point to aid overall team focus.

Bruce believes that the use of a few fundamental management tools is vital to overall organization success. Because managers at all organization levels devote so much of their time to dealing with daily issues, sticking to the basics is critical. Using the Mission Statement as a guide, a plan is developed to establish a road map for required action.

Dynamic Plan

This plan included business results expected and individual objectives for executive managers and professionals. Once the plan has been reviewed and finalized it becomes a living guide with periodic checkpoints. This follow up is the most critical aspect of the process, which creates a spill down affect throughout the enterprise. At each checkpoint each staff member presents results to their manager and the managers present the combined results to the executive staff. Heavy emphasis is placed on the measurement of these results and updates or contingency plans are openly communicated.

This proactive approach insures that efforts remain on track and areas are identified where planned results may not be met so that corrective action can be initiated. Contingency planning is an integral and ongoing aspect of their performance management process so that adjustments to changes in direction or projects that get off track can occur in a timely fashion. The discipline gained is woven through the daily operation of the business to maximize overall success.

Building Skills

In tandem with operating effectiveness, is continuous improvement of staff quality through a concentration on hiring the best people and investment in skill development. Bruce believes that the interaction between staff motivation and intelligence/skills is the multiplication of these two factors to derive expected results rather than addition. He has found that an emphasis on both is critical to long-term success to avert over reliance on either side of the equation. (e.g. 0% motivation x 80% intelligence/skill=0 results).

The concluding principle he utilizes is a pragmatic mix of written and verbal communications where project or plan details are documented however discussions are held before plans can be finalized. Again, over reliance on either reduces the quality of outcomes. He cited the example where a member of his management team was recommending investment in a technical venture which was Internet related. The initial verbal presentation created a very exciting impression yet a review of written details raised numerous questions, which were reviewed in subsequent discussions. The decision he and the manager reached was not to proceed.

Bruce continues to guide the shift in organization management style from a more traditional command and control approach to one where a greater emphasis on coaching/delegating is practiced. The change is driven by a combination of his organization philosophy and changing workforce expectations. This highly mobile and increasingly independent nature of today's technical professionals has significantly impacted the need for change.

The management model being implemented employs an emphasis on a match between business demands or individual motivational needs and the leadership's pattern which will maximize results. He coaches his staff who in turn lead their team toward a continuous assessment of the stage of organization development achieved which determines the most effective leadership model to employ.

The driving force to aid the change process is a continuously improving performance management system including clearly defined follow up check points to insure progress towards goals remain on track. The underlying guide empowers each individual so that they can be provided the maximize level of independence based on the capability level of each individual performer. Bruce believes that the successful implementation of these techniques will significantly impact future success of their business.

We can now meld the pragmatic applications with historical theories and research create a workable view of the keys to organization success. Even though these basics are simple and fall into the category of "common sense", they are often extremely difficult to implement because the essence of the organization is "social" rather than" mechanical".

8

SOCIAL CONNECTION

Our travel through the centuries, reviewing the study and functioning of the organization has provided a fresh prospective on practices that have worked well and many which have long outlived their usefulness. What is most striking about the Chief Executive case studies is the consistency exhibited in several areas of organization developments. The essence of the organizations depicted or observed throughout history is that in all cases they are a <u>social</u> unit that binds people together in a variety of ways to accomplish some end. Often this fact has been overlooked or ignored resulting in an emphasis on structural, systems, or process related characteristics of the unit. This has been particularly evident from the Industrial Revolution to the modem era.

Historical snapshot

Our study of the prehistoric clan brought out the natural development of individual role definitions and the highly organized aspect of all their endeavors. Woven throughout all their activities was constant social interaction, which greatly aided their survival in an extremely hostile environment and facilitated skill development to bring them success in each clan duty. Most critical tasks such as hunting, food gathering, cave selection were completed as a team effort with obvious social connection.

Our close genetic cousins, the chimpanzee, demonstrate similar patterns of social behavior with very natural abilities to organize most activities. Their ability to learn sign language, use tools, and navigate through dense jungle is impressive and has been recognized by many scientists as proof of the link between man and the chimp. The group interactions documented provide solid evidence that the foundation for most organization units is primarily social. In addition, the theories developed and research conducted by Rupert Sheldrake further supports the realization that most animal species demonstrated a natural predisposition to coordinate and organize their behavior in groups. Some of the earliest recorded examples of the next stages of organization evolution existed in ancient Greece, Rome, and Middle East. These very early, more formalized organizations, were formed to support the practice of religious belief and coordinate military campaigns. Plato was one of the first to describe many organization roles and he identified the critical characteristics of a successful leader.

During the early formation of Israel as a country, King David established one of the earliest centers of trade and commerce in Jerusalem. A historical review of these organizations from several different perspectives bring out two critical factors affecting the viability of these ancient social units. In most cases, there was a charismatic leader who became a catalyst for the formation and direction of the unit and those actively aligned with the organization exhibited a strong sense of purpose and loyalty. As we have all observed, most of today's religions were founded during this period, demonstrating significant growth and survival. Also, the military conquests of the ancient Greeks and the Roman empire are significant examples of organization effectiveness. Early descriptions of formal organizations were included in the works of historians, poets and the writers of religious text.

As the physical sciences become more formalized fields of study, the roots of the social sciences were formed. Applying scientific techniques to create a better understanding of society and human behavior formed the foundation for anthropology, sociology, and psychology. This application of scientific techniques led to tools that were later used to identify and measure organization dynamics and results. The historical viewpoint we have taken allows us to see organizational phenomenon that was previously overlooked because it was not the object of defined study until very recently. This includes culture, leadership, management structure (e.g. bureaucracy) and loyalty. Out of the social sciences has evolved the extensive study of public and private sector organizations.

Peter Drucker targeted the 1950's as the period when the concept of the organization as an object of study was clearly defined. The watershed event leading up to the period was the analysis of the Hawthorne Studies which enhanced general awareness of basic organizations dynamics. Many of the elements identified by social scientists were now being recognized within the industrial environment. Douglas McGregor defined two primary management views of worker motivation. The Theory X description identifies a need to control and push people to meet very rigid expectations while Theory Y paints a very positive picture where people have a fundamental desire to contribute meaningful results that lead to organization success. Frederick Herzberg applied the Theory Y theme, theorizing that work performed is the most powerful motivator for achieving needed results versus hygiene factors such as money, status, or work environment.

Peter Drucker has been recognized as one of the prime architects of the Management By Objectives (MBO) process, which continues to this day to be considered a critical management tool. He remains a long term advocate of this Performance Management process including an organization Mission Statement, long range goals, specific measurement of required results, and detailed objectives that captured needed operating results to ensure organization viability and effectiveness.

Warren Bennis was one of the first theorists/practitioners to move away from the use of bureaucratic controls toward a flatter more flexible organization structure. This was also a significant feature Peters and Waterman observed during their study of highly successful companies.

Chief Executive Applications

It was obvious that all the Chief Executives that chose to contribute to this book had incorporated most of these organization principles highlighted into their leadership model. They all have internalized a significant number of the fundamentals discussed and clearly viewed their use as critical success factors. None of them cited organizational techniques that gained popularity in recent years (e.g. reengineering) and stressed the successful application of a few basics as critical to organization effectiveness. An understanding that the social elements of their enterprise formed the foundation for leadership success and continuous assessment utilizing systematic tools to analyze effectiveness were clearly evident. Each demonstrated a theory and viewpoint describing management priorities and recognized that a significant aspect of their leadership role was the formulation and communication of high priority goals. They understood that people wanted to know where the organization was headed and their role in achieving desired results. With this sense of purpose and meaningful, challenging and satisfying work assignments they were confident that the entire social unit would exhibit sustained energy and positive activity leading to the expected results.

The entire group had successfully implemented a highly effective Performance Management program which was fully integrated into the business planning process. For the most part, the key components stressed by Drucker and numerous other MBO enthusiasts, were in place. It is a very interactive process with a continuous upward, downward and lateral flow of information. This has led to high levels of understanding, agreement and commitment where the entire unit is moving toward results in a coordinated fashion.

In all cases, the use of all of these methods reinforces a participative approach to organization direction. Where feasible, staff members are asked to propose their contribution to planned operating requirements and become involved in potential changes or critical decisions. The expectation that everyone at all levels will champion actions to support the needs of customers and recommend vital improvements is constantly reinforced.

Conclusions Reached

Throughout most of my career, I have remained a strong advocate of participative management supported by the expectation that most people will try to accomplish needed results if provided effective guidance and leadership. When I began this project, I had no idea that the scientific and historical study would provide such compelling evidence that these principles could create such a powerful foundation for maximizing organization success. This consistent theme re-occurred as our study progressed and was reinforced by the Chief Executive Case Studies.

In order to create a workable model from the depth of work captured in this book, I have condensed this foundation into critical pillars classified as the "4 P's".

- Purposeful Action
- Participation for All
- Performance Management for Results
- Precision Throughout

Purpose

This factor has been at the core of most surviving and successful organizations throughout history. Whether it is our animal cousins, prehistoric clans, early social units, or modern enterprises, this sense of purpose has been very evident and critical to long-term results. Early religious groups demonstrated missionary zeal, military units rallied to great causes, scientists and philosophers have been in search of prime cause and fundamental truth, nations have been formed to accomplish citizen's dreams, and companies have thrived because of flawless customer satisfaction.

Recognized purpose has been the cohesive influence that binds members as a unified force. It generates focused action, unwavering loyalty and well-coordinated efforts. Drawing a parallel to physics, it acts as gravity which focuses all organization unit participants on a common cause.

Participation

Most species including humans throughout their evolution have clearly demonstrated a very natural propensity to organize their activities. By simply getting individuals involved in a unit's planning and decision making process a very powerful cohesive and interactive force is unleashed. This stood out as one of the most significant variables that impacted Hawthorne's study results. The basic issue to be considered by organization leaders is "who's in control". George Milne stressed the importance of the Hawthorne affect and Ray Sansouci viewed control as a pivotal issue for most organizations.

For those who have practiced participative management techniques, they consistently experience a higher level of commitment to accomplish required results and self-directed behavior. Human resources are much more effectively utilized with this involvement and most operations tend to be more pragmatic and efficient. The further leaders dip into the unit to provide design input the better the finished structure will function.

The force created from this approach is analogous to the electromagnetism that exists throughout the universe. It drives the interactive power and provides needed connectivity. Techniques have been developed and many approaches to participative management have been utilized which successfully tap this powerful resource. Successful channeling of this power can result in a highly effective structure and operating capabilities.

Performance Management

The strong channeling force that can be put into play to focus and connect organization components is a pragmatic, flexible performance management process. Numerous examples are cited throughout this work which has demonstrated the power of this leadership tool.

The key components discussed include clearly communicated purpose (mission statement), organization wide development of targets of opportunity (goals), bottom up/top down agreed upon objectives to implement goal attainment, periodic checkpoints to track results and shift priorities, and final review of results for designated periods of time. This mechanism creates energy, coordination, and the measurement to maximize results. In concert with our physics model this would emulate the strong nuclear force.

Precision

With all these other critical components functioning effectively, the follow-through and actual execution of required actions rounds out the model for organization success. Most critical to the achievement of desired results is clear, consistent measurement of target accomplishments. Time must be devoted to the development of well understood metrics throughout any operating unit that leads to up front agreement between those delivering the results and other who lead or monitor achievements.

This feature was taken to the extreme by Taylor, refined by McGregor and Drucker within the MBO process, and utilized by Crosby's TQM methodology and reengineering efforts. This common element, if consistently and pragmatically applied, will ensure organization success.

These benchmarks provide clear targets for desired results and greatly increase the prospects the precise delivery will occur. It is this consistent meeting or exceeding agreed upon standards that is a mark of true quality and customer satisfaction. This could be viewed as a weak nuclear force to conclude our grand unified physics model.

9

SCIENCE BRANCHES REUNIFICATION

o o o o o o o o o o o o o o o o o o o o o o o o o o o o o o o o
"You can't depend on your judgment when your imagination is out of focus."

—*Mark Twain*

During our historical journey to identify critical factors leading organization success, we witnessed the evolution of science and formation of various specialized branches. The social sciences have provided the bulk of the framework for study of the organization yet many other scientific principles have been imbedded in these components. Dr. Milne, President of Pfizer Central Research, referred me to two-time Pulitzer Prize winner, Edward O. Wilson who has argued for a unification of all fields of knowledge. His guidance in this area has definite relevance to our efforts to gain a better understanding or organization effectiveness.

In his book *Consilience* (Wilson, 1998) he has led the search for consilience which provides proof that everything in our world is organized around a few fundamental natural laws that comprise the principles underlying every branch of learning. Similar to this historical exploration he draws from the physical sciences, biology, anthropology, psychology, religion, philosophy and stresses goals from the Age of Enlightenment as a foundation for his work. To achieve the consilience of physical science with social sciences and humanities, he believes that educators should stress commonalties between the various branches to all students.

Professor Wilson's well-supported theories of social behavior strongly reinforce the evidence presented throughout this book that most living species are predisposed to organize their environment and activities. Leading scientists and philosophers from the Enlightenment era were empowered by excitement of discovery and a strong belief that science could reveal an organized, understandable universe. These great thinkers believed that the elegant precision of the celestial bodies discovered by astronomy and physics could provide a model for human society.

He also states that our Neolithic ancestors demonstrated continuous curiosity, creativity, and the natural ability to organize critical aspects of their existence. This directly supports a critical thesis of this book in that a historical review of the evolution of the organizations demonstrates this innate ability of most species to effectively organize their social existence. He believes that the human attainment of high intelligence and culture stands out as a highly critical step in the overall history of life.

Wilson further contends that the main failing of the social science branch is the lack of a true social theory which has been a barrier to communication with the natural science. There are four features of a sound theory to bridge this gap. They include parsimony where units and processes to explain the phenomenon are minimized, generality that maximizes the range covered by any model, consilience, and predictiveness in results of test by observation and experiment.

Modern Theory for Organization Effectiveness

In the spirit of the Enlightenment era and consilience, I have chosen the Grand Unification theory developed within the field of physics to create a framework for a modern theory of organization effectiveness. Brian Green, an eminent physicist at Columbia, has provided an exceptional historical account of the study of the universe in his book

The Elegant Universe (Green, 1999). Most physicists have been searching for a model that identifies the critical forces that interact in a unified fashion to explain the interworkings of the universe. Professor Green begins his description of this theoretical interaction between the four primary forces of nature with a relative ranking of their strength.

He begins his discussion stating his amazement with the huge range exhibited in each of their intrinsic strengths. Electromagnetic force is proportionally only 1% the strength of the strong force while the weak force is a thousand times weaker than electromagnetic measurement, and gravity is a hundred million billion billion (million (10^{35})) weaker. Recent research has established a clear connection between strong, weak, and electromagnetic forces and the underlying role of gravity has been established by scientists for over 400 years.

In addition, scientific studies have proved that electrical attractions between oppositionally charged particles and gravitational attraction between bodies of physical mass get stronger as distance decreases.

A very delicate interaction exists between these primary forces of the universe. (Polkinghorne, 1996) Electromagnetism, the key to chemical bonding, is at the optimum strength to find chemical compounds and greater strength would cause a slower rate for chemical reactions causing the evolution of life to be greatly retarded. If the strength of electromagnetism to gravity were only slightly stronger, stars would be too cold to support life and if slightly weaker a star's life span would be significantly reduced, negating evolutionary history to develop on planets.

The balance of the two additional forces of the universe is equally delicate. Weak nuclear force that causes matter to decay has been critical to the early evolution of nature. Slightly greater strength and galaxies would have condensed while slightly less strength would have brought about the destruction of hydrogen immediately after the "big bang." Strong nuclear force holds nuclei together and a similar imbalance would either destroy hydrogen or the ability of stars to burn. It ensures the correct mix of carbon and oxygen, the very essence of life as we know it.

Organization Balance

Creating a measurable balance of the Four P's that mirrors this Unified Theory can provide a very usable/testable theory for organization effectiveness. A proper balance between each can be designed and evaluated to establish the architecture to maximize success and staying power for any organization. If any one of the four components is missing or at ineffective strength an organization's functionality will diminish. The greater the balance and match with required strength of all four, the better the resulting overall measurable effectiveness.

A formula representing the combination and interaction of these factors can be developed to create a base line for study and analysis.

$$E = f\, P(wu + wa + wm + wr)$$

Where E is the measure of resulting effectiveness when adding the specific measures of all four P's (P̲urpose, P̲articipation, Performance M̲anagement, and P̲recision). They will receive the appropriate % weight (w) based on the most workable proportion for each factor.

It is the creative balance between each of these critical factors that provides maximum organization effectiveness. Through the measurement of the force associated with each, the proportions can be evaluated and fine-tuned.

Expected Force

Just as observed with gravity, a sense of organization purpose is the most subtle of the four forces that comes into play to drive results. The extent to which everyone associated with a unit understands and accepts their connection to the common purpose determines the gravitational center for the organization.

Because of the basic nature of this factor, there is a tendency for organization leaders or designers to usually assume that this organization gravity will exist without a defined consentration on its creation.

There are numerous examples throughout history where the force has either clearly existed or has been absent. A direct link has been shown between the level of common organization purpose and effectiveness. Any leader leaving this development effort to pure chance will usually have a serious short fall in this critical area.

Therefore, several highly effective elements should be employed to create organizational gravity. These include a clearly defined set of critical success factors, a bottom/up synthesis of an understandable purpose for the unit, and a well-defined strategy to focus efforts. These elements should be combined into a communication package that is presented to all organization levels both verbally and written.

The methods used to develop this roadmap are extremely critical and greatly influence the overall effectiveness of the message.

One of the most successful developmental techniques is to bring a critical cross section of organization leaders together to focus on the primary mission of the enterprise. In the profit sector, the classic determination is "What Business are We In." If the majority of these leaders have a highly participative style the quality of current information used in the defining process is greatly enhanced. A thorough review of this question to achieve consensus on the answer will lay a solid foundation from which to build a center of gravity. This process also works very well in the public sector by a shift in focus to the critical service being provided to a clearly defined constituency. The use of business terminology and management techniques can achieve similar results even if the profit element is not relevant.

The definition developed becomes the corner stone of a clearly articulated strategy which becomes an essential roadmap for action. Organizations that do not group the basic nature of their business or lose sight of the target usually experience deteriorating results. One of classic historical examples are the Railroad Companies that missed the fact that they were in the Transportation Industry. Theoretically, they could have been at the leading edge of trucking and air travel.

The most important elements of the strategy are a small number of clearly articulated Critical Success Factors and well defined strengths that drive success. These create a backdrop for the listing of prioritized actions required and projected measures for success. This document should be kept as brief as possible and highly dynamic.

In addition, leaders who define businesses focus and develop strategic direction should identify high priority values that can be recognized across the organization as guides for action. Alignment of these values with those exposed by a significant cross section of the organization will further strengthen the potential cohesive force. A summary of these components can form the basis of a high impact presentation that is communicated at all levels and periodically reinforced. This message when combined with actions consistent with the key principles articulated, create organization gravity.

If properly orchestrated, this creates a cohesive force to hold the organization together and align unit actions. Similar to force identified throughout the universe, this subtle force gains strength as the mass of the organization grows.

The physical state cause by gravitational force that is most observable and has direct impact on our environment is inertia. The range of examples is extensive but a few are stopping a car, lifting weights, or moving a large piece of furniture. Ironically, one of the most commonly observed social occurrences is described as "organization inertia". It is most often cited when companies are intent on implementing change of are highly satisfied with a very effective operational process. This parallel reinforces my use of the physical universe as a model for organization design and development.

The extent to which those leading and/or designing organizations develop and reinforce the basic purpose for any unit will directly affect the gravitational force within the organization. As observed in the study of the universe, the strength of this very subtle force can increase to a phenomenal level as the size and scope of the organization expands. Gravity allows density contrasts to grow, leading to the emergence of structure (Rees, 1997). It leads to the formation of differentiated structures, which drives cosmic evolution and creation of "self-organizing systems".

The proper balance of organizational gravity establishes a platform for continuous growth and expansion of organizations. It interacts with the three other key forces to maximize alignment to ensure overall effectiveness.

Staff Involvement

Throughout history there has been a slow but steady migration toward a greater depth of staff involvement in the charting of organization mission and decisions that determine critical actions. The bulk of this shift occurred during the last 20–30 years based on the recognition that involvement leads to significantly better results due to greatly enhanced staff commitment. The critical issue is the degree to which top leaders believe they need to hold power and authority. Several factors impact the level of control chosen including an unconscious inclination to use command and control management, belief that only senior management has the skills to properly structure an organization, or distrust of the basic motivation of mid management and first line staff.

Evidence abounds that living organisms including humans are very proficient in organizing their activities. Since the beginning of recorded time humans have formed organizations and the majority of their primate cousins do the same. Leaders of modern organization are much more attuned to recognizing the power of this great historically untapped resource.

The challenge has always been to develop techniques and programs to gain the optimum level of staff involvement. Organization size tends to be the variable that has the greatest impact on success in this area. As the business grows the ability to gain optimum involvement diminishes. Leaders who make the effort can reap tremendous results through use of bottom up planning and project management and a collaborative decision process.

Most businesses have some form of business planning to guide day-to-day management of the enterprise. Adding a real time component to the planning process that focuses on how the business is organized and work is processed can provide a very powerful mechanism for continuous change and structural enhancements. Given the opportunity, individuals at all levels of organization can demonstrate their commitment and depth of understanding of basic organization principles. The goal for most enterprises is the creation of a self organizing capability that consistently refines, modifies, and/or renews how the organization operates.

Two recently published books provide very compelling evidences that humans are fundamentally committed to achieving positive outcomes and self organization has occurred very naturally throughout history. Matt Ridley, eminent scientist and editor for the *Economist*, developed a thesis that humans are impelled to live in cooperative, complex societies. His book *The Origins of Virtue* stresses that morality existed before the Church, social contracts before Hobbes, and welfare before the rights of man (Ridley, 1996). He demonstrates that evolution has led to the human capacity for social trust which is as vital a form of social capital as money is a form of actual capital.

Fritzof Capra, Director of the Center for Ecoliteracy, in his book, *The Web of Life*, synthesizes many recent scientific breakthroughs relating to the study of all levels of living systems (Capra, 1996). He maintains a common ingredient that exists across all fields of scientific study is an understanding of organizing relations. His research further reinforces much of the evidence cited thus far in this book that living systems demonstrate a pattern of self organization.

If there were any remaining doubts concerning full utilization of this natural resource, these works put them to rest. Including a feedback mechanism from organization staff concerning organization structure, processes, and critical initiatives, can be a powerful tool to effectively establish a truly participative management model. Organization leaders need to select the method that provides the best feedback loop for them yet the planning component I have suggested stands out. It provides a pragmatic method for gaining the electromagnetic connectivity which can be readily implemented into the ongoing growth and change process for the enterprise. What follows is a recommended approach for the creation of this self-organizing capability.

Fritzof Capra describes a self-organizing system as the spontaneous emergence of new structures and new forms in open systems far from equilibrium, characterized by internal feedback loops. (Capra, 1996) The development and integration of a feedback mechanism that incorporates input from the bulk of organization members into the planning process can become a powerful regeneration tool.

One of the key factors included in the organization message presented to the organization is a brief description of how the planning efforts support enterprise success. In addition, how their input into this effort greatly enhances overall success and the ongoing nature of the process.

Each organization then needs to determine a workable method to gather participant feedback on the following:

- How each individuals role aligns with the "big picture" mission.

- What are the most significant issues affecting overall business success.

- What procedures, methods etc. are working well or need improvement.

- Suggested improvements to improve operating results.

- Other factors that each organization determine to have a significant impact on the optimization of organization effectiveness.

It would be ideal if this feedback mechanism is developed based on impact from all organization levels. This will insure that information gathered will provide valuable guidance to alter organization structure, methods and direction.

An example of a technique that has been successfully used by marketing professionals for years is use of guided focus group meetings. As long as these groups include a representative sampling of all segments of the organization, the data gathered can be very powerful. A survey can be developed for completion on-line could be another approach to gather this useful data. There are numerous methods that can be tailored to provide the information desired and each organization should select the approach that fits their needs best.

The developers of the operating plan can use the data to conduct a gap analysis to identify potential areas for improvement or change. Product developers could begin to communicate directly to customers rather than link through marketing. Sale professionals may develop individual sales projections rather than getting a top down quota mandate. These potential organization modifications are fed back to everyone providing the information for confirmation prior to further modification and inclusion in projected plans.

The completed plan including the organization enhancement segment is presented as previously outlined.

This model can also be used to develop and implement other significant changes such as new computer systems, new site selections, or product implementation. The natural capability to effectively organize activities will become increasingly obvious and the electromagnetic energy created will strengthen organization connectivity and bonding.

Performance Management

An effective Performance Management program is the strong nuclear force that insures focused action and maximum organization alignment. Over the last several years MBO has lost favor in many segments of industry due to ineffective utilization of several basic principles. Implementation of all critical components will overcome key deficiencies and highly focused results will occur. Properly balanced organization gravity and electromagnetism created by a clearly stated mission and participative organization leadership should include defined goals as general targets designed to guide long-term success. These goals act as focal points to channel more detailed requirements stated as objectives for projected results. Several examples include:

- Significantly increase market share for all major products in each global region.

- Consistently lead the market in the development of new or enhanced products.

- Attract and retain organization staff that demonstrate capabilities that place them in the top echelon of their market peer group and continuous performance improvement.

Many readers will be very familiar with numerous other examples of these ongoing, consistent guides that act as pillars for required results.

The stage is now set to include performance management as a vital element of the business plan process. To the fullest extent feasible, each individual is asked to develop a set of draft objectives that will prioritize activity during the defined planning period. Each objective will describe the action required, the measurement of the result, estimated cost when appropriate, and time to completion.

For example:

- Identify a new market nitch for database software which will increase market share 2% by 12/01. (Cost: $50,000)

- Develop next upgrade to database software product designed to reduce cost 20% by 6/01. (Cost: $75,000)

In essence, each individual becomes a cost center and a potential profit center. They review draft objectives with their manager and the two revise as necessary until they agree on required results. Each manager completes a similar exercise with their manager where their objectives incorporate targeted results for their unit plus individual objectives. This roll up process continues up through all organizational levels.

Managers play a critical role as facilitators of the performance management process. They help prioritize actions, draw out creative ideas, and guide development of written objectives. Throughout history bureaucratic structure has been instrumental in the submersion of new concepts and has retarded needed change. One of the most significant principles of the Blake and Mouton leadership model is that ideas are drawn from all work group members to insure that group decisions result from a thorough review of all possibilities.

The level to which individual objectives are developed will vary across a wide range of organizations. In some cases, first line production supervisors may use worker input to develop objectives for the work group and this designated leader carries the process forward. Other comparable groups may use a similar method.

With today's technology all resulting documentation should be developed and tracked on a computerized system. As discussions progress, revisions are easily recorded and when ready the plan is finalized. Results are tracked by individuals and reviewed by work group managers in a dynamic, timely manner. This paperless process further strengthens the effectiveness of the system.

The most critical factors that impact the success of performance management are clear measurements and continuous review of results. An ability to quantify projected results at all levels is crucial to the creation of this strong nuclear force resulting from effective performance management. Use of a sports analogy where everyone knows how to keep score and the actual score at each phase of the game is easily understood by all participants. I will expand this further during my discussion of organization precision. In addition, periodic check points need to be established to determine if priorities have changed and the progress toward planned results.

The target dates and review process at each of their check points need to be established when objectives have been finalized. Ideally, this review will take place every 2–3 months and each individual understands that they are responsible for triggering the process. They develop a summary of results and schedule the discussion with their manager. The manager should be prepared to discuss potential shifts in priorities that could require new or revised objectives and completion dates. All updates are then documented and the next review target is established.

These fundamental techniques insure that performance management continues as a dynamic driving force for the organization. It acts as a strong nuclear force which results in optimum organization alignment and complete focus on high priority results.

Precision

This is the last of the critical forces that has an influence on the organization similar to weak nuclear force that completes the linkage demonstrated in the unified theory for the physical sciences. The use of math to measure early economic, scientific and financial endeavors began to appear in several early civilizations dating back to 2000 B.C. (Aczel, 1996). Babylonian engineers and builders began to compute areas and volumes and scientists were able to estimate ratios. A farmer's success was usually dependent on the area available to grow crops.

Pythagoras is recognized as an early historical figure that formalized and developed a substantial body of mathematical knowledge. He and other mathematicians such as Archimedes demonstrated the use of math as a tool to propel technical advancements.

As society evolved, mathematicians continued to perform a pivotal role in the development of more advance social and military technology. The ability to precisely measure commercial applications such as exchange rates, profits, and costs become critical to the advancement of mercantile society. This early development and use of math became the model for scientific advancement (Aczel, 1998).

Galileo measured the movement and organization of the universe, Newton established physics as a science and defined gravity, Hubble discovered expansion of the universe, and Einstein established the foundation for unified force theory. The key to each advancement throughout history has been our ability to calculate the interaction of variables and establish mathematical proof!

The ability to project quantifiable measures for desired results provides a powerful mechanism to focus actions and generate feedback on actual outcomes. The level of specificity required for scientific research need not be achieved by most organizations yet each should agree and clearly communicate requirements. Several of the CEO case studies provide usable examples of a measurement mentality.

George Milne has measured a culture at Pfizer Central research where everyone is expected to test assumptions and look for patterns with a sense of restless curiosity. Jack Blaeser instills the use of pragmatic financial indications to chart results all functional areas of Concord Communications. All strongly advocate the use of measurable objectives to align the organization and focus actions.

Each individual developing a performance plan needs to understand and be well trained on methods to measure results. Well communicated and fully understood quantifiable measurement parameters throughout the organization is a tremendous asset to ensure consistent plan development.

Examples of these measures include dollar amounts, per cent improvement, ROI or time to complete tasks. Throughout history math has been a form of language which can be applied very successfully to promote alignment in the modern organization.

This measurement mentality creates an environment where results are increasingly precise and continuous improvement is achieved. Consistent delivery on commitments made to customers significantly differentiates any business from their competition.

Well aligned focus on clearly understood targets with consistent delivery that hits the mark is truly the ultimate critical success factor. This becomes the final organization force that parallels the weak nuclear force which completes the link of organization effectiveness to the unified physics model.

10

EFFECTIVENESS MODEL

We are now faced with a challenge to effectively measure and calibrate the balancing of the 4 P's. There are a wide range of assessment tools available that can be tailored to determine the actual level of each force operating in the organization. To guide this process, a model needs to be developed to capture the perceived power of each from a representative sampling of organization members. The technique that I have chosen is the administering of a questionnaire that develops a ranking of organization effectiveness variables that fit within each defined category.

The following is a list of the defined variables:

<u>Goal Setting:</u> Employees work toward clear objectives which fit in with organizational as well as personal career goals.

<u>Feedback:</u> There is good two-way communication between managers and employees so that both sides are informed of employee performance.

<u>Responsibility:</u> Employees are given enough authority to do their jobs and the freedom to determine how best to do them.

<u>Participation:</u> Employees are encouraged to participate in making decisions, to speak up when they disagree with their bosses, and to make suggestions.

<u>Leadership:</u> Managers provide vision and inspire commitment to quality and productivity by stressing excellence in everything that is done.

<u>Teamwork:</u> The work is organized so that employees can work as a team and/or freely exchange ideas and opinions.

<u>Coordination:</u> There is communication and cooperation, rather than competition, between different groups in the organization.

<u>Standards:</u> The organization demands high quality work and insists that employees at every level give their best effort.

<u>Reward:</u> Pay, benefits and promotions are administered well. Employees who do their jobs well are rewarded.

<u>Recognition:</u> Employees who do their jobs well are recognized for their efforts.

Each variable is aligned with one of the P's:

**Purpose**	_**Participation**_	_**Performance Management**_	_**Precision**_
Feedback	Participation	Goal Setting	Standards
Responsibility	Teamwork	Coordination	Rewards
Leadership			Recognition

The raw score ranking for each variable provides a new measurement of force and the weight that exists for each category. These calculations are applied to the formula discussed earlier: $E=f\,P(wu+wa+wm+wr)$

The maximum weight average raw score for each force measured by this questionnaire is 45 and the maximum weight is 100%. The following is an example of the resulting calculations:

$$E=29.2\%(35)+20.8\%(25)+33.3\%(40)+16.7\%(20)$$

$$E=32$$

Based on these results we can draw some conclusion about the organization.

- Effectiveness is 71% of potential. (32/45)

- Purpose and Performance Management forces are relatively strong.

- Participation and Precision forces are relatively weak.

- The force levels for all P's are reasonably balanced.

Additional measures can be compared to the variable weight of the 4 P's to determine optimum balance. Financial data used to benchmark within industry segments can be utilized for this calibration (e.g. profit margin, market share, annual revenue growth) and tracking the correlation between business results and organization effectiveness level plus the balance of the 4 P's.

The best method to examine my proposed theory would be the use of techniques developed by astronomers. Through the use of consistent financial measures to identify the brightest stars, a survey can be completed to determine effectiveness level and balance. Correlation of this data will establish the validity the measured effectiveness and determine which weighting mix of the 4 P's is most powerful.

Organization leaders may determine that a more focused study will provide meaningful data. Focus group discussions to review survey results should provide useful insight that may calibrate the most effective balance of the four forces. In addition, programs can be developed overall effectiveness ratings which then can be correlated to financial data.

This model is similar to quantitative decision methods that guide a wide range of organized activities. The ability to make use of information gathered to determine probability outcomes is extremely valuable (Aczel, 1998). System Theory techniques have been utilized very successfully to demonstrate how different equation variables interact and determine potential results.

Amir Aczel puts forth a very strong argument that equations developed to measure natural phenomenon demonstrate underlying rules of nature. It is my belief that this model emulates this principle.

EPILOGUE

The challenge now becomes selection of a testing method to validate the 4 P's model. After brainstorming a variety of techniques with executives from a wide range of industry segments we settled on an approach utilized for years by population polling services. Just as astronomers use powerful telescopes, we used a targeted questionnaire completed by a small random sample of organization employees and the capture of company financial data. A basic correlation of these data sources should demonstrate the power of organization forces to generate positive business results. Just as Hubble revolutionized our view of outer space, this study has similar potential to unlock mysteries of organization effectiveness.

Early in the 20th Century, Hubble discovered an intriguing phenomenon resulting from his astronomical observations. There was a consistent, curious light shift observed indicating that a vast majority of stars were moving away from earth. This led to his hypothesis that we exist in an ever-expanding universe (Hawking, 2001). His work became the corner stone of scientific research that led to Big Bang Theory outlining the origin of the Universe. Previously, physicists believed that the universe was static and today a large segment of this scientific community believes that it continues to expand because of the effects of the "big bang" beginning.

The utilization of basic polling techniques to emulate the astronomers telescope, shows definite potential for similar understanding of our global universe of organizations. Upon completion of the Organization Effective questionnaire by a small random sample of target organization employees, we are able to establish a measure of force for the 4 P's. Through a comparison of these forces to key measures of business success such as profit margin and revenue growth, the impact on effectiveness can be demonstrated where high effectiveness scores will link to increased levels of success.

In similar yet less explosive fashion than the "big bang", the human organization originated in small geographic region and has expanded to the world population we know today. A recent scientific study of the current human gene pool confirms that the human race originated in Africa and expanded out of Africa to most regions of the world. (Nature, 2002) The researchers found that a significant portion of our current pool is directly linked to the earliest know Homo Erectus fossils and conclude that we survived over other early human species because of our propensity to socialize and assimilate. It is a natural element of our drive for survival to ban together in communal groups and this tendency to cooperate underlies the resulting assimilation. The proof of this theory was based on the analysis of the modern human gene pool which is remarkably homogeneous and demonstrates that major population expansion resulted from interbreeding, not replacement. It can be concluded that the formation of organization units is a natural evolutionary outcome of this tendency to cooperate rather than dominate and the primary elements of the organization are social rather than structural.

Astronomers have crafted a scientific analogy where galaxies are to astronomy what ecosystems are to biology (Rees, 2001) and consistent with the spirit of E.O. Wilson's consilience theme, ecosystems can be compared in similar fashion to economic industry segments. One of the historical figures discussed earlier, French father of Sociology Auguste Comte, also took an interest in astronomy and mused that science would never be able to analyze the chemical structure of stars. This not only supports Wilson's thesis but further demonstrates the potential connectivity between physical and social sciences. Ironically, within a few years, Newton demonstrated that sunlight could be split into spectrum and display all colors of the rainbow. This discovery led to techniques used to analyze colors emitted by glowing gases to determine the chemical make up of stars.

As many cosmologists continued to develop proof of an ever expanding universe, two radio astronomers from Bell Labs discovered the residue of the big bang. The expansion of the universe which originated with phenomenally intense heat required many years of cooling to reach the current temperature. Researchers have found that this afterglow of creation emits the radio waves discovered by these two Bell Labs scientists, Penzias and Wilson. This discovery has been critical proof to the existence of the originating explosion which created our universe and the expansion measured by Hubble. The resulting evolution of stars and galaxies has been shown to parallel the development of biological systems where a trend toward greater complexity and differentiation is exhibited.(Rees, 2001)

We can extend this analogy further using a research comparison between the study of organization dynamics and the explanation of our expanding universe. The "background radiation" available to provide a snap shot of the "big bang" that began the evolution of the human organization is included in volumes of anthropology and archeology research data. The results provide a clear image of early social units and the study of a variety of civilizations that function as prehistoric societies further bring this image into view. This includes clans living in South American rain forests, Australian outback, remote artic regions, or jungles in the orient.

It is this experimental foundation that has been demonstrated throughout the historical progression tracked thus far. When coupled with the organizational analysis model described in the last chapter, a very powerful, easily implemented tool can be utilized to validate the powerful forces demonstrated by the 4 P's. To test this organizational analysis model, a number of companies were approached to elicit volunteer study participants.

To facilitate the process, several simple steps were used to complete the study. Each participating organization designated a study coordinator who was asked to select a small random sample of employees (roughly 2%) and each received an email with a 50 question survey enclosed. Prior to receiving the survey, the study coordinator explained the scope and purpose of the study and they were asked to return the completed survey directly to me. When all the completed responses were received, the raw score for each category was calculated along with a total across all categories. From this a ranking for each category was developed plus a resulting percentage of the total potential raw score.

Each organization also provided the percentage increase in revenue and profit before tax for each of the previous three years. This average percent was then correlated with the survey average percentage for all four factors to determine the link between the four key organization forces and business results. The study successfully demonstrated that the model was workable and can be utilized to provide specific organization effective feedback and further test the validity of the 4P's hypothesis. The initial results for a very small sample of organizations demonstrated a positive relationship between survey score and financial data where those with higher positive survey ratings had better financial results.

The following is an example of the feedback presented to one the participating organizations. The overall effectiveness rating for your organization is 70% and the only comparable norm at this time is the American Customer Satisfaction Index which has average 72.5% favorable over the last 4 years. Our plan is to establish norms for this study model and we will update you when a reasonable sample level is achieved. The highest ranked effectiveness category for your organization was Participation based on a positive sense of involvement with the company mission and open, effective communications. Ranked second was Purpose due to a well defined focus on a clear Corporate mission resulting in solid staff commitment to achieve company goals. Next is Precision where an emphasis on good quality results exists and follow through on critical success factors is expected. The lowest ranked category is Performance Management because longer term operating objectives are not clearly established and individual career goals not well defined. Internal competition appears to be more common than mutual cooperation in daily operations. Improvement in this category would have the most significant positive impact on your effectiveness rating percentage and initial results of our organization effectiveness study show a positive link to business results.

Readers are encouraged to further test this effectiveness model using a questionnaire of their choice that measures the force of the 4 P's or my instrument. One critical goal of my work is the stimulation of further study to test my hypothesis that the 4 P's are the primary forces that drive fundamental organization effectiveness. As additional organizations are evaluated, the resulting correlation will prove or disprove this theory. The evaluation and increasing force of the four organization pillars within the context of historical evolution can significantly impact measurable organization results.

A recently published book, *NonZero* (Wright, 2000), which traces the evolution of human culture, identifies a similar set of pillars that have driven the advancement of human society. In parallel fashion to my work, Robert Wright describes the relentless advancement of human culture from the prehistoric era through major historical periods to current times. He also draws of research from most major branches of science and also stresses the consilience theme.

He makes a compelling argument that a driving force leading to the advancement of human society has been the ongoing effort to invent or imitate new methods to enhance quality of life (e.g. hunting, scavenging, foraging, fighting). He points to the first solid evidence of human culture as being the discovery by archaeologists of crude stone tools and contends that natural selection favors genes for innovating, observing, imitating, communicating, and learning. This built in sense of purpose became a self-feeding process causing progressive cultural evolution which is in direct alignment with the first P.

This sense of purpose demonstrates that human history and evolution are not aimless but has basic direction where biological evolution created complex, intelligent animals and through cultural evolution the human species is pushed toward greater social complexity. Humans have a natural propensity to organize their surroundings and actively influence social success and survival. This "co-evolutionary" advancement is caused by genetically based human assets which have led to stunning cultural achievements. The mass of humanity over the ages have carried life to increased levels of organization where individuals at all levels of social strata were active participants in the evolutionary process. The natural competition between individuals or social units has always encouraged long-term integration. Robert Wright believes that "cultural evolution long ago supplanted genetic evolution as our key adaptive mechanism".(pg. 296) Thus, a clear linkage to the second P is established.

The critical tool that provided connectivity to social units has been information-processing technology which created the level of development required for the functioning of a formal organization. Globally, the formation of complex societies has been connected to the recording and transmitting of information. Early examples include writing, drums, delivery of messages on horseback, and the recording of information on scrolls. Later advancements were the printing press, telegraph, recordings, and telephone which greatly increased the range and speed of information flow. As this technology advanced, the size and complexity of social units moved on a parallel evolutionary path which led to improved organization administration. Large continuous land empires, formalized religion, and global business enterprises were all possible and required human efforts could be planned, implemented, tracked and rewarded. This historical advancement is directly aligned to the third P.

Wright's primary thesis defines the overall direction of historical evolution, from the earliest discovered life forms to current space travel, as having developmental direction rather than aimless movement. He presents evidence for his position utilizing a fresh look at a vast array of scientific exploration. Social survival, evolutionary success, and the positive direction of historical evolution directly support an intrinsic drive for precision by living organisms and social units. This success depends on results driven activity throughout history with a propensity toward the selection of workable methods over ones that do not lead to positive results. This is the last pillar in Wright's evolutionary model and can be directly aligned to the 4th P.

Focus on the Organization

The primary deficiency which has led to poor organization results throughout history has been the lack of leadership focus on the fundamentals of organization effectiveness. This can be traced to a variety of causes such lack of knowledge, focus on organization structure rather than culture, bias against the consideration of social factors, or other related dynamics. It has been my intent throughout this work to paint a clearer picture of the historical evolution of these fundamentals and pragmatic techniques that can support positive applications. We can only speculate, at this point, how a better focus on organization effective might have further influenced social progress and reduced social disruption throughout history.

It is very important that the simplicity of this effectiveness model does not deter further testing because many have recognized that the application of the basic forces is not easy! I encourage each reader to use their natural curiosity and test the application of the "4 P's" in their organization, work group, community group, or family unit. It is my sincere hope and expectation that proof will result to support or disprove the hypothesis presented. This exploration can be conducted at all organization levels because the fundamental power of understanding exists within each of us.

The testing methods can include the study of organization dynamics, historical analysis, works of fiction/nonfiction, political events, or completion of scientific research. One painful example similar to the WWII incident described in the Introduction, are the events leading up to our 9/11 disaster. During the period, a war existed between two different organization styles where US agencies such as the FBI, INS and CIA are bureaucratic, lacking aligned missions with extensive political infighting. Terrorist organizations are organic, well aligned globally with a clear common mission. If a survey were conducted to measure the 4 P's which would have the higher score? A similar study could have been conducted comparing WorldCom/Enron prior to their collapse to Pfizer and Microsoft. Based on my personal knowledge of these latter two companies, the results are obvious to me.

The excitement generated from the quest for a better understanding of our universe moves forward. Very recently astronomers announced that the most detailed and precise map yet developed of the universe at its birth had been completed. New satellite technology was used capture a picture of the universe 200 million years after the Big Bang and computer simulation then modeled the evolution over the last 13.7 billion years within a 1% error margin. Scientists involved believe that the foundation has been laid for a unified theory of the cosmos. This provides further reinforcement for those of us who continue to study our organizational universe that similar findings are within our reach. We can draw inspiration from students throughout history who believed that clear linkages exist between physical and social science that will verify visionary theories.

Most importantly, please accept the caution also stressed in the Introduction and do not become captives of jargon, media touted fads, sexy structural models or the latest rage. Rather, focus on the fundamental "blocking and tackling" of organizational leadership. The process of developing this book over the last eight years has been one the most enriching experiences of my life and was clearly motivated by my drive for "self actualization". May each of strive for similar experiences.

BIBLIOGRAPHY

Abercrombie, Nicholas, Hill, Stephen and Turner, Bryan. Dictionary of Sociology (New York: Crown Publishers, Inc., 1989)

Aczel, Amir. Probability 1 (Orlando: Harcourt, Inc., 1998)

_____ Fermat's Last Theorem (New York: Dell Publishing, 1996)

Adler, Mortimer. Aristotle for Everybody (New York: MacMillan Publishing Co. Inc., 1978)

Armstrong, Karen. A History of God (New York: Ballantine Books, 1993)

Auel, Jean. The Clan of the Cave Bear (New York: Crown Publishers, Inc., 1989)

Beardsley, Monroe (Editor). The European Philosophers from Descartes to Nietzsche (New York: Random House, Inc., 1960)

Berlinski, David. A Tour of the Calculus (New York: Vintage Books, 1995)

Blake, Robert and Mouton, Jane. The New Managerial Grid (Houston: Gulf Publishing Company, 1978)

Cahill, Thomas. How the Irish Saved Civilization (New York: Doubleday, 1995)

Capra, Fritzof. The Web of Life (New York: Anchor Books, 1996)

Crosby, Philip. Quality Is Free (New York: The New American Library, Inc., 1980)

Cummings, L. and Scott, W. (Editors). Readings in Organization Behavior and Human Performance (Georgetown: Irwin-Dorsey Ltd., 1969)

Drucker, Peter. Innovation and Entrepreneurship (New York: Harper & Row, 1985)

Etzioni, Amitai (Editor). Complex Organizations (New York: Holt, Rinehart and Winston, 1961)

Ehrenreich, Barbara. Blood Rites (New York: Metropolitan Books, 1997)

Fouts, Roger. Next of Kin (New York: William Morrow and Company, Inc., 1997)

Green, Brian R. The Elegant Universe (New York: W.W. Norton & Co., 1999)

Goodall, Jane. Through a Window (Boston: Houghton Miffin Company, 1990)

Hammer, Michael and Champy, James. Reengineering the Corporation (New York: Harper Collins Publishers, Inc., 1993)

Hawking, Stephen. A Brief History of Time (New York: Bantam Books, 1988)

_____ The Universe in a Nutshell (New York: Bantam Books, 2001)

Kaplan, J.D. (Editor). Dialogs of Plato (New York: Washington Square Press, Inc., 1951)

Matteson, Michael and Ivancevich, John (Editors). Management and Organization Behavior Classics (Boston: Richard D. Irwin, Inc., 1993)

Peters, Thomas and Watterman, Robert. In Search of Excellence (New York: Harper & Row, 1982)

Polkinghorne, John. Beyond Science (Cambridge: Cambridge University Press, 1996)

Rees, Martin. Before the Beginning (Reading, MA: Addison-Wesley, 1997)

_____ Our Cosmic Habitat (Princeton: Princeton University Press, 2001)

Ridley, Matt. The Origins of Virtue (New York: Penguin Putnam, Inc., 1996)

Sheldrake, Rupert. The Presence of the Past (Rochester, Vermont: Park Street Press, 1995)

Templeton, Alan. "Out of Africa again and again", Nature (London: Macmillan Journals, March 7, 2002)

Weber, Max. The Theory of Social and Economic Organization, trans. Henderson and Parsons (New York: Crowell-Collier Publishing Company, 1964)

White, Michael. Isaac Newton (Reading, MA: Addison-Wesley, 1997)

Wilson, Edward O. Consilience (Thorndike, Maine: Thorndike Press, 1998)

Wright, Robert. NonZero (New York: Pantheon Books, 2000)

0-595-27132-4

Printed in the United States
23318LVS00006BA/130-135